AS FOR ME
AND MY NATION

―――― *Sandy Bates* ――――

Published by **Sandy Bates**
Copyright © 2023 Sandy Bates

All rights reserved. No portion of this book may be reproduced in any form without permission from the publisher, except as permitted by U.S. copyright law.

All Scripture quotations (unless otherwise stated) are from the New King James Version of the Bible. Copyright © 1979, 1980, 1982 by Thomas Nelson, Inc., Publishers.

Cover by **Rebecca Bates**
Edited by **Ashley Bates**
Interior Design by **Rebecca Bates**

ISBN (paperback): 979-8-9887018-0-4
ISBN (hardback): 979-8-9887018-1-1
ISBN (ebook): 979-8-9887018-2-8

Printed by Amazon.com, Inc.

First Edition

TABLE OF CONTENTS

Endorsements	v
Foreword	xi
Introduction	xiii
As For Me And My Nation	1
──1. *My Beloved America*	1
──2. *The Arising of the Army of God!*	13
──3. *Can These Bones Live?*	43
──4. *Restoring Our Voices*	58
──5. *The Third Day Era*	85
──6. *Choosing Greatness*	117
──7. *Gathering Together on the Wall*	135
──8. *The Tale of Two Towers*	145
──9. *The Day of the Prophets*	177
──10. *Riding on the Mountaintops with Jesus*	192
──11. *True Liberty*	207
──12. *The Rebirth of America*	229
Bibliography	251
Acknowledgements	259

Ruthann Miller

This book is such a timely word for this hour as deception is at its all time high like never before in history! As you read it, your spirit will come alive and be awakened to the truth. It will rouse you to speak out God's truth from His Word through decrees and declarations into the atmosphere while influencing those in your sphere to hear what the Spirit of the Lord is saying to His people as a whole, not just for our nation, but for every nation.

For such a time as this, we are rising up from the ashes with renewed hope, leaning on our Beloved, and taking back territory where the enemy has stolen from us. As you read and meditate on each page that is written by this chosen scribe, you will hear the cry of God's heart to His children to come alive and walk in their divine calling and purpose, for the Harvest is ripe and white, awaiting us to receive them.

In His Service,
Ruthann Miller
Founder and Creative Director,
Sisterhood of Grace

Ruth Saw

I do not know anything about American politics, but I love how Sandy used various stories in the Bible to encourage us to rise up to be His salt and light for our nations. She cleverly reminded us through His Word and her prophetic insights that we have the victory! Indeed, I declare, as for me and my nation, we shall SEE the glory of God!

Ruth Saw
Author & Founder,
The Clarity Expert

Hacksun & Seya Cha

What a joyful book! The powerful message in this book reminded us of our memories from several years ago.

From early 2017 on, hundreds of thousands of South Koreans poured out into the streets to do one thing: cry out to God to save our country South Korea from the enemy.

It turned out that a wrong person took the office of president by using fraudulent methods. When many Koreans realized that the wrong one not only took the presidency but planned to turn our country into something like North Korea, people made a decision to cry out, "This is wrong, the false one must go," and they filled the streets of the Gwanghwamun Square in Seoul. (This movement is continuing to this day.)

We were two among them in the streets, crying out to God to help us and save our country. It was a hard season in which we were not sure if our country could really be saved or if it would be forever gone. Many people said it was the biggest crisis ever since the foundation of the country, apart from the Korean War. It was a life-or-death situation for our country. (Perhaps you can relate to our situation.)

However, sometimes God uses the devil's attack to do something good and surprising.

One night at the end of 2019, in the streets of Seoul where hundreds of thousands of patriots gathered in an overnight prayer rally, we received the baptism of the Holy Spirit. We didn't even know there was such a baptism until that day. We were desperately crying out to God to give us anything to save our country, then the language we spoke changed from Korean to a heavenly one! I am sure there were many who received the same gift on that day.

Fast forward to 2022, and we now have a new president, legally elected by real people, without election fraud. Those people who stood against the evil investigated, monitored, and did everything they could to prevent election fraud. The enemy did attempt to steal the election again, but this time God intervened, and the attempt failed. Hallelujah!

After all those troubles, which are still ongoing, so many Koreans were equipped with knowledge of conspiracy, fraud, and other schemes of the enemy, more than any other time in history. Many realized that we must take our land back!

We realized that many people, including us, were sleeping spiritually until we saw our country in a dire situation—as dire as becoming like North Korea. When the church is sleeping, the enemy is skipping the church and playing. When many people finally woke up, cried out to God, made a voice for truth, and took risks by taking action against evil, God honored us and brought changes in our country.

God also did something new in our lives. We're writing this in South Africa, not South Korea, because after all those events God launched us as missionaries traveling all over the world, leading tens of thousands of people to Jesus. It is our best season yet.

What has God done? In short, God used a dire situation to pull us out and send us to a destination He set for us. God had to bring us onto a cold asphalt to cry out to Him because the cold asphalt was our launching pad.

In this book, I found the following declaration, which came true in our lives:

> *"What has seemed to be like our worst season is actually going to lead us to our best season!"*
> Chapter 12

Sandy is our dear friend, who we met in an online school. She is a really good person, you can tell, but what God hid in her heart is unshakable loyalty, which was revealed through a dire situation regarding the U.S. presidential election. When Trump's second term was stolen, many were disappointed, but some were appointed to do something.

In 2021, we joined a Zoom prayer meeting with Sandy and other friends. When we prayed, I (Seya) saw in my vision that Sandy was a giant (a spiritual giant in God, nothing like Goliath). She was standing among mountains that looked smaller than her. Her movement was slow since her body was huge, but when she swung a sword one time, all the enemies were killed.

One year after the vision, I received this book. This means her sword was finally swung!

Although the subject of this book is very serious, we were filled with joy and even burst out laughing so many times when reading it. Our hearts were ministered to so pleasantly as we read. The book was so inspiring and encouraging that I (Hacksun) found myself prophesying over me and my nation.

Several days after reading, we realized that the vision I saw for Sandy being a giant among mountains and swinging a sword is not only for her but for many who will read this book.

When you wake up and walk in God's will, you will realize that you are actually a giant among mountains and have a sword in your hand. You will realize that by the sacrifice of Jesus Christ, God gave you power to destroy the enemy, and all the mountains are for you to take!

We find this book is full of love and impartation that will empower you and prepare you to step into God's victory and the destiny God has set for you and your nation.

Now it's time for you to be a giant. It's time for the enemies to be killed. It's time for you to take the mountain(s)!

We believe that through this book many readers will rise up as spiritual giants. We believe that through many of God's giants God will restore and even rebirth America. Just as Sandy wrote, "Our best days are yet to come!"

We appreciate what Sandy has done in this book. We honor what God has done through her. We bless this book, and we pray God will lead readers into a place of victory, in Jesus' name!

Hacksun & Seya Cha
Traveling missionaries from South Korea

Foreword

    Sandy's passion for the Lord and for our country comes through every page of *As for Me and My Nation.* She does an amazing job of addressing the Church of Jesus and the issues of the nation while weaving together testimonies of personal encounters with the Lord. This is not an easy task! Sandy has put her heart, soul, and life into being able to relay the message that has been burning in her spirit for years.

    I have walked out much of the journey of writing this book with Sandy. We first met in our *Writing in the Glory* classes, led by our writing mentor, Jennifer Miskov. Immediately, Sandy's passion for the Lord to be lifted high in her life, the church, and our nation became evident. It continued to fan the flame that God had ignited in me for similar issues. As I took over leading Jennifer's classes for a season, it was such an honor to help Sandy in the process of writing this book. I can assure you that she has wrestled with God through fears and questions that all new authors face and has overcome each hurdle by the overcoming power of Christ! She did it because she answered the call for our nation to turn back to Christ—one person, one family at a time.

As for Me and My Nation is not just another book! It carries a fresh anointing for us to *see the Lord arise over His church and this nation!* As you read this work, pray for eyes to see and ears to hear what the Spirit of God is saying to you in this hour. Ask Him what to do with what you hear. I am convinced that Sandy—along with every one of us—has been brought into the kingdom for such a time as this (Esther 4:14). We must answer the King of Heaven's call!

Sandy, it is an honor to call you friend. It is exhilarating to see how you have persevered and pressed into the high calling that the Lord has for you. I cannot wait to see what the Spirit of God does with you and with this message.

America, it's time for hope to arise!!!

Gabby Heusser
President of Gabby Heusser Ministries
Author of *In His Footsteps* and *Deeper Still*

INTRODUCTION

I write this book first to the Church in the United States of America. It is impossible to address the nation of America without addressing the Church in America. Jesus said to His people:

> *You are the salt of the earth; but if the salt loses its flavor, how shall it be seasoned? It is then good for nothing but to be thrown out and trampled underfoot by men.*
>
> Matthew 5:13

We are the salt of America, and if we are not *being and speaking* as salt, we will lose our flavor and be trampled underfoot by men. What does that mean to be trampled underfoot by men? Simply put, if we don't wage a good fight in the Spirit (in prayer and allowing our voices to be heard), then we could lose the right to have a voice, because losing certain religious freedoms could cause us to be trampled underfoot by evil men. We shouldn't let that happen!

We have been in a tremendous shaking in our nation that has been exposing corruption many of us didn't know existed. The battle has been between good and evil. Our nation was founded on biblical principles, and Godly men and women dedicated this nation to God; however, a corrupt, antichrist agenda has come into play that has tried to steal our God-given purpose and destiny.

I also can't write this book to the Church in America without addressing the rest of our family around the world. We are one body of believers in heaven and on earth. We have one Father and we also have one main enemy, the devil. The devil may look and act a bit different depending on where you live, but I like to say that although the devil likes to put on different costumes depending on the party he is attending, he is still the same, ugly devil underneath the costume using the same evil tactics. Therefore, we are fitly joined together in heaven and earth, and Father God sees us as one body. We are truly His family and His kids!

> *For as the body is one and has many members, but all the members of that one body, being many, are one body, so also is Christ.*
>
> 1 Corinthians 12:12

— Introduction —

I have been so touched and so grateful at the number of believers around the world praying for our nation. I would like to thank our family around the world for standing with us during this trying season. We are also standing with you for your battles. I believe some of our battles right now have been very similar, if not the same; there have been antichrist agendas coming against God's people, including whether we can keep basic God-given freedoms like our freedom of religion and freedom of speech. I'm reminded of the scripture:

> *Rejoice with those who rejoice, and weep with those who weep.*
> Romans 12:15

America has been in a battle over whether we will be able to keep certain liberties that our country was founded on. Because our nation has been a leader of the free world, most people realize that if we went down, there would be a domino effect on other nations that depend on us to carry the torch of liberty. On the flip side, however, our victories will be your victories because America has been known for promoting liberty and human rights around the world.

Lastly, it is impossible to address the Church and the nations without addressing how this affects us individually, along with our families. You will see in this book that I have laid out spiritual principles of warfare that will give us victory on a personal and family level, on a Church level, and on a national level. I truly believe that our finest hour is ahead of us, and we need to run for the prize that is set before us. This prize will be one of liberty and destiny in Jesus!

— How This Vision for this Book Began —

It was the day after our 2012 presidential election. I was on my way home from taking my kids to school, feeling a bit downtrodden and disappointed because the candidate I voted for had lost. I had not been particularly fond of our conservative choice this time, but at least he represented many of our values (or so I thought). However, as I mused on the way home and spoke with the Lord, I felt God was saying that this was for the best, because of the *better plan* God was going to do in the next election. I didn't know what that better plan would be yet; however, I sensed that somehow God was taking the sleeping in this nation to the end of themselves so we would realize our need for God's intervention. Then one day shortly after this, I was in prayer and heard myself boldly declare, "**As for me and my nation, we will serve the Lord!**"

As I mentally replayed what my mouth had just said, I realized that I had just prayed Joshua 24:15 with a new emphasis. The verse actually reads, "*…As for me and my **house**, we will serve the Lord*," which I had prayed many times for my own family, as I'm sure many of you have also done, but I never had prayed that in a national way before, nor do I remember hearing it prayed that way. As I contemplated this declaration over our nation, I believe the Lord started showing me a strategy for victory concerning the political and spiritual battles we are facing. God began to give me a new vision and hope for America, especially concerning the role that God's Church would play in this victory.

I had originally intended to call this book, "*As For Me and My Nation, We Will Serve The Lord.*" However, during a prayer time at a Christian conference in the fall of 2018, I heard the phrase, "*As for me and my nation, we will SEE the Lord.*" As I meditated on the change from "serve" to "see," I felt the Lord was giving me a prophetic promise that He is going to show up in this nation in a mighty way that we will SEE! Also,

— Introduction —

I believe the change in this phrase better depicts our New Covenant in Christ. In the Old Covenant, we were servants, but in the New Covenant we have been made sons and daughters (2 Corinthians 6:18)!

In the story of Lazarus in John 11, Jesus spoke to Martha and encouraged her to believe that He could raise Lazarus from the dead. I believe that what Jesus said to Martha, He is saying to us:

> *Jesus said to her, "Did I not say to you that if you would believe you would **see** the glory of God?"* (emphasis added)
>
> John 11:40

I believe this is a promise to the Church in America and around the world: stand with God and believe that we will *SEE HIS GLORY!*

My Beloved America

Chapter 1

It was the beginning of 2016. I was having one of my regular prayer times on our back deck. This time I was praying for our nation, the United States of America. It had been obvious for some time that we were in a battle over our destiny. While I was praying, God's words of promise bubbled up in my spirit, giving me fresh hope and vision. I knew this message was to God's Church in America and around the world, to be in agreement with God and partner with His great plan for our land. God wants to give His Church a new vision for the future of America. This beautiful message I received in prayer is as follows:

My Beloved America:

How I have loved you with an everlasting love, says the Lord. How I have fought for you. How I have protected you!

Your latter shall be better than your former. Your end is more blessed than the beginning. I will pour out my Spirit once again on this great land. Your sons and your daughters shall prophesy.

Speak to the mountains that are before you and speak my grace to them. Know there is power in My Name. I have given you My Name.

Know that nothing, nobody, shall be able to stop the outpouring of My Spirit on this land once again. Don't believe the discouraging lies of the enemy. There are more for you than against you.

My Name shall be great in this land once again, says the Lord who loves you!

I am completely convinced that God loves this nation very much. I feel in prayer His love for this country. I have also heard messages from reliable prophetic voices in which God addresses this nation as "My America." The devil has already lost the battle of stealing this nation from God and His people, and we will see the evidence of that in the days ahead.

Our assignment as a nation is not over, but just beginning. We have an anointing and assignment to promote the gospel around the world and also promote liberty and human rights. Our best days are yet to come if we the Church will continue to arise and take our places as His salt and light in this nation.

I believe this is a new day of power for God's Church in this nation and around the world. I believe our days of sitting on the sidelines are over: God is personally commissioning us to move in greater authority and confidence in Him. After all, the earth belongs to the children of God:

> *The heaven, even the heavens, are the Lord's; but the earth He has given to the children of men.*
>
> Psalm 115:16

God and all of heaven are rooting for us. The earth is waiting for the revealing of the sons and daughters of God (Romans 8:19). Let us not disappoint, but run the race God has for us:

> *Therefore we also, since we are surrounded by so great a cloud of witnesses, let us lay aside every weight, and the sin which so easily ensnares us, and let us run with endurance the race that is set before us, looking unto Jesus, the author and finisher of our faith, who for the joy that was set before Him endured the cross, despising the shame, and has sat down at the right hand of the throne of God.*
>
> Hebrews 12:1–2

God is not only the author and finisher of *our* faith, but He is the author and finisher of our *nation*. I believe God is saying that we will finish in victory, not defeat. Believe that all things are possible with our God!

The Beginnings of a Great Nation

Never underestimate small beginnings (Zechariah 4:10). A foundation of destiny was laid by a group of Christians called the Separatists in the early 1600s. Along with the rest of the Pilgrims, they traveled thousands of miles cramped together in horrible conditions on a ship called the Mayflower just because they wanted to have the freedom to worship God in a way that was true to their beliefs. Most of them were probably just trying to survive; starting a nation was not even their goal, let alone helping to create one of the greatest nations on earth. Even the planting of the cross on that fertile soil in Virginia by English settlers thirteen years prior to the Pilgrims, which might have seemed insignificant to many, played an important role; their prayer of dedication over this land is something God has recorded in His Hall of Faith! God doesn't ever forget our prayers. He also doesn't forget or let go of something that any group of people willingly dedicated to Him. And when most people may be tempted to forget, God does not ever forget the precious prayers of His children; He remembers His covenant promises over His people. The vials of prayer begin to tip over!

Our nation has been one of the most blessed nations on earth despite our very young age. From countless inventions, scientific breakthroughs, and medical cures, our nation has prospered greatly. Throughout our nation's history, our country has considered itself a primarily Christian nation, and prayer has been welcome in our public settings (mostly until recent years). We have seen great awakenings and revivals for Jesus in our land. Our nation has sent out tens of thousands of missionaries around the world, along with sending the gospel through television into most of the world. We have been an advocate for human rights in many nations and have fought wars to set others free. We have not been a perfect country; we did things that were seriously wrong at times. However, God has honored the remnant that has confessed His name over our country, and God has brought necessary corrections and justice when we have strayed from Him. There has always been a remnant church in our country to cry out for justice and righteousness and revival, and God has always been faithful to answer our prayers!

As a nation we have enjoyed one of the best political systems in the world based on a "We the People" style republic. However, many of us have been shocked to see communist and socialist agendas being pushed by very left-wing organized groups of people in this nation. History shows us that these types of governments have never worked and never will because they are not based on Godly values. It is denial and self-delusion to think that any country can thrive and prosper if you take away individual freedoms and God-given rights. One difference between a socialist type government and a democratic republic is the liberties given to the individual. Socialism/communism wants to control from the top, and most of the time, this ends with individual liberties and wealth being taken away from the people to support the top. God wants everybody to win; therefore, a democratic republic style government is based on "we the people" and should be a win-win for everybody when it works at its best. Our constitution is based on Godly values because individual rights and liberties are valued. This is how God treats all of us; He gives us freedom to choose between right and wrong. He wants us to choose Him and reap the rewards of Heaven, but He will respect our choice to spend eternity away from Him if we don't choose Jesus as our Savior.

We have been in an obvious season where the devil has tried to destroy the liberties and freedoms that this nation began with. However, when we turn to God (and we have been), God will do a mighty restoration and give us great recompense.

—— How My Passion for America Began ——

I haven't always had a passion to pray for our country—or even to pay attention to politics. I really had not paid much attention at all growing up. There was no particular tradition in my home for a particular party; I just remember my parents voting for who they liked. Therefore, I liked who they liked but didn't give it much further thought.

I gave my heart to Jesus at the age of eighteen and began attending a large, charismatic church in a suburb of Atlanta, Georgia. I remember one day our pastor was admonishing us that it was our Christian responsibility to vote. *Vote? Vote for who?* I thought. I didn't know much of anything about politics. I didn't know the difference between any of the political parties or what they stood for. They were all the same to me, and they seemed rather boring. I would have known who the President of the United States was, but honestly not much past that—maybe not even who the Vice President was! It would have been quite embarrassing if Jesse Watters, a political commentator known for his man-on-the-street interviews, had shown up with a microphone asking me political questions; I would have been clueless. (Of course, Jesse Watters would have been a young child then!)

However, since I was an obedient type of church-goer, I made sure I stood in line to vote since I was told to. In typical Pharisee fashion of keeping this new law of voting without caring about the reason voting was important, I went to vote just to say I voted. Seriously, I had no idea what was going on, nor did I do any research. (In my defense, that was before we had the internet, so research would have been a lot of work!) I'm pretty sure most of the time I just looked over the list and picked whoever in no particular party. Maybe I liked the sound of their name, maybe I had actually seen an advertisement and they seemed nice—who knows? I was obedient: *check!*

It wouldn't be until many years later that I really cared about who was elected in governmental positions. For me, it was the natural progression of adulthood, which included raising a family and *paying taxes*, that began to wake me up to the fact that the leadership of your country is a factor determining the quality of your life and the future of your children.

My journey of awakening to the sense of urgency to pray for our nation began, for the most part, during the Obama Presidency. It is not that I didn't occasionally pray for our country before; however, this was different. Like many of us, I noticed that this nation was taking a sharp turn to the left, away from many of our biblical, conservative values. I was deeply concerned over the extreme rise of abortion, the redefining of marriage, declining patriotism, deep state corruption, etc. The rise of political correctness had attacked our freedom of speech and religious liberties. We began to see lawsuits against business owners simply for declining to do something that violates their religious beliefs. We soon began to see the rise of the cancel culture where you can be canceled and censored on all sorts of media platforms because of your opinions and personal beliefs. This was not the America I grew up in.

It was during this time that it became increasingly clear to me that there was a spiritual battle taking place in our political sphere that was important for God's people to fight in prayer along with our voices. Many Christians have been taught that it is not important for God's people to engage in political battles. However, my husband, Jim, wisely pointed out that it would be fine for us to stay out of the political arena if the devil was not there, but since our enemy has declared war in the political arena, then we have to answer the call to fight back. The devil always wants the high places that control culture, and we shouldn't let him have that place of influence!

I continued to work on this book on and off for over a decade before finishing in the summer of 2023. To be honest, it was a spiritual battle to complete, but God brought so many faithful friends and family to intercede for me and encourage me. There were times that I thought I had missed my timing on this, but God was faithful and reassured me that the timing was in His hands. Most importantly, my vision and passion for the message of this book grew and matured in my heart as I continued in prayer for our nation along with thousands of others in the Body of Christ across this world. I realize now that the awakening had to occur in myself first in order to adequately express what God was showing me.

The vision I was seeing in 2012 was just the beginning, however, as it grew dramatically as the political landscape in this nation changed in a way that many of us didn't see coming. The miraculous election of Donald Trump in 2016, who is a true patriot for America and a champion for the cause of God on this earth, was an intervention of God which I will explain further in chapter six. However, most of us didn't anticipate the level of warfare we would see come against him and anyone who stood with him. As I am writing this, we are still in the thick of this battle.

The Beginning of a New Decade

We recently entered a new decade in 2020. Many have noticed and commented that 2020 reminds us of what the medical field considers to be good vision. When I first thought about having *new vision* in the beginning of 2020, I was excited and full of anticipation for what the Lord would do, as I'm sure many of you were also. I had heard one of my favorite ministers, Pastor Hank Kunneman, prophesy that this would be a "decade of light"[1] and also "a decade of difference." However, he did say in one of his prophetic words that the decade would start out harsh, and boy, do we know how that has been true!²

It is interesting that the devil seems to know when God is about to do something really awesome: he starts a counter attack which is usually the *opposite* of what God is promising us. That in turn gives us an opportunity to press into God in order to stand in faith and not get discouraged just because things seemingly are going contrary. Usually according to how big our promise is, the enemy will launch a sizable attack to throw us off.

Therefore, this decade started out harsh with a pandemic called COVID-19 that hurt and killed many people. Many churches were pressured to close their doors and quarantine when God's Church should have been a light and hope during that dark season. Some government leaders labeled the Church non-essential when we are the *most essential* in my opinion when those around us are hurting. I believe the enemy tried to use this pandemic to separate us during a season when we needed unity more than ever. However, for myself and many others, God turned that into a miracle, as I met many Christians around the world whom I am now great friends with just because many Christian groups went online for their meetings.

The Hebrew year for 2020 was 5780, which began September 30, 2019, since the Hebrew New Year begins approximately three months before the Gregorian calendar. The Hebrew letter for 80 is "pey," which is symbolic of the "mouth." I believe this is going to be known as a "decade of speaking" in which our words are going to be anointed by God to bring hope and wisdom to a world hungry to know Him. Therefore, it is not by accident that the enemy did an *opposite* and caused the last few years to include wearing face masks and practicing social distancing. Just know as a rule of thumb that what God is planning for His people is *always* way better than what the devil is destroying. God is planning to put a spirit of boldness on His Church like never before, using our voices mightily. Jesus is the lion of the tribe of Judah, and we are going to be like Him, and we are going to be a roaring group of lions in His tribe! The Bible says in Proverbs 28:1, *"The wicked flee when no one pursues, but the righteous are bold as a lion."*

I believe this is a decade and a season of allowing God to perfect our vision for what is possible with Him. This is a time of awakening, a time of clarity, and a time of great hope! I believe God wants us to have a new vision for our country, the United States of America. He also wants to do the same thing for His Bride around the world who are believing for their countries also. God is in the process of a great reformation and awakening—politically, economically, morally, and over God's Church. God wants you to also have a new vision of yourself! See yourself winning!

Though the battle is raging, God is encouraging us that He has a plan to take back this country for Him, and He will not disappoint! In Romans 8:31, the Bible says, *"What then shall we say to these things? If God is for us, who can be against us?"* I believe God is saying to His Church in America and around the world:

> *For I know the thoughts that I think toward you, says the Lord, thoughts of peace and not of evil, to give you a future and a hope.*
>
> Jeremiah 29:11

Moving Forward

As we begin this book, I encourage you to touch your eyes and ears. Ask God to give you ears to hear and eyes to see. God wants you to see clearer in the Spirit than you ever had and hear the sound of victory clearer than you ever did.

We were made to walk as kings and priests on this earth (Revelation 1:6). God wants to do exceedingly, abundantly, more than we can ask or think in our nation and world.

You will see in this book that I will highlight several Bible stories in which we get an example of how to fight the current battles we are in. I believe we are in the day when we will see many of our favorite Bible stories come to life for us. Just like God would fight the battles for Israel and bring them great deliverance as they cooperated with His instructions, I believe God is having His Church cooperate with Him to win the battle for this nation! To be on God's team is always the winning team, so no worries; we've got this!

In this book, whenever I refer to the "enemy" or "enemies" in the context of present-day battles, I'm referring to the devil and his demons. The Bible makes it clear that our battle is not against people, but against principalities and powers of darkness. Yes, demonic spirits work through people; however, we want to pray for and love people, fighting against dark forces by prayer and by making stands for God.

> *For we do not wrestle against flesh and blood, but against principalities, against powers, against the rulers of the darkness of this age, against spiritual hosts of wickedness in the heavenly places.*
>
> Ephesians 6:12

Also, when I refer to "deep state" in this book, I'm referring to corrupt politicians or leaders in various areas of society that are doing illegal activities to harm our nation or the people of this nation. There are many good politicians and leaders which we honor and are grateful for. We should pray for God to remove the corrupt leaders and to give us righteous ones in their place.

Even though I'm addressing the United States of America in this book (since it is the country I live in), this also applies to the Church around the world. We are all one body and one blood in Jesus, and we stand with each other for the God kind of liberty in all of our countries! We are standing together for a world-wide revival. May God richly bless you with wisdom, revelation, and encouragement as you read this book!

THE ARISING OF THE ARMY OF GOD!

Chapter 2

> *To everything there is a season, a time for every purpose under heaven:*
>
> *Ecclesiastes 3:1*
>
> *A time to love, and a time to hate; **a time of war**, and a time of peace.* (emphasis added)
>
> *Ecclesiastes 3:8*

For several years now, I felt the Lord highlighting the word "arise" to me in my prayer times. I wasn't sure at first what He was saying. I would ask the question in my heart, "Arise to what?" At first I thought it was something I needed to *do*, which is certainly part of it, but now I believe it is more about *positioning* myself. Let me explain:

The word "arise"[1] means:

—to get up from sitting, lying, or kneeling; rise
—to awaken; wake up
—to move upward; mount; ascend
—to come into being, action, or notice; originate; appear; spring up
—to result or proceed; spring or issue (sometimes followed by from)

The way I interpret this for our purposes as the people of God is that we need to *"change our position."* If we are lying down on the ground feeling powerless and defeated, we need to *get up* and know who we are in God—that if God is for us, who could be against us (Romans 8:31)? If we are asleep to what God is saying and doing, we need to *awaken* ourselves and ask God to open our eyes and ears. To move upward and ascend would be to pray, get in God's presence, and see things from His perspective, which is higher than our perspective. Isaiah 55:9 says, *"For as the heavens are higher than the earth, so are my ways higher than your ways…"* To come into being or action would be to move in our callings and destiny, knowing God has equipped us to do whatever He has called us to do. To proceed would be to move forward—put our hand to the plow and don't look back (Luke 9:62). The common theme in all these definitions of "arise" would be to change our position from a place of defeat to a place of victory!

> *Shake yourself from the dust, arise;*
> *Sit down, O Jerusalem!*
> *Loose yourself from the bonds of your neck,*
> *O captive daughter of Zion!*
> Isaiah 52:2

The above scripture implies that *we* have the power to loose ourselves from the bondages of this world and of the enemy (the devil). Like Sampson, the power of God within us can shake any bonds off! The point is, we are free, yet we don't know we are free. Whom the Son has set free is free indeed (John 8:36)! The cage of life we are in has been opened, and yet, we are sitting behind the bars believing we are still in bondage.

Dust in the Bible usually denotes a sense of "humanness" since we were created from the dust of the ground (Genesis 2:7). However, as a child of God who has accepted Jesus as our Savior, we have now been made sons and daughters of God (Galatians 3:6). We are royalty; we are now kings and priests of God (Revelation 1:6). We have been given the power from Jesus to bind and loose on this earth (Matthew 16:19).

> *Behold, I give you the authority to trample on serpents and scorpions, and over all the power of the enemy, and nothing shall by any means hurt you.*
>
> Luke 10:19

One of the biggest lies of the enemy is to make us *feel* unworthy to be powerful in God. The devil loves to remind us of every mistake we have ever made whether it was *really* a mistake or the devil just told us it was. I personally have a very sensitive conscience, and it is not hard to guilt me over the slightest thing; therefore, it is an area that I personally have to work on in God to resist the tendency to be too hard on myself.

The truth is that the enemy is very afraid of the Church. Jesus has given us authority in His name. The big truth is that Jesus *already* paid the price for every sin or mistake we have or will ever make when we have made Him our Savior. Jesus, like a good parent, just wants us to learn from our mistakes and move forward with Him. In Disney/Pixar's movie, *Finding Nemo*, a character named Dory responds to her friend's anxiety by telling him to "keep on swimming." Likewise, we just need to keep moving forward toward our destiny in God.

The Bible says in Proverbs 24:16 (emphasis added), "*For a righteous man may fall seven times and* **rise again**, *but the wicked shall fall by calamity.*" I love that scripture because that means we get unlimited chances to get something right that we keep failing at! Seven is a perfect and complete number in the Bible, which means we can fall again and again and still get back up. That is why Jesus told Peter to forgive seventy times seven (Matthew 18:22); He was emphasizing that we should forgive again and again! For the wicked, however, it is a different story. They must get born-again to be able to receive forgiveness for their sins (Matthew 3:3). Otherwise, though God is merciful and long-suffering, giving people a multitude of chances up until they pass away, their time of judgment will come if they refuse to receive Jesus.

The devil will never get a second chance, and he is a bit upset and bitter about that! Sometimes, if the devil is accusing and criticizing me, with those fiery darts he likes to throw at our minds, I like to turn around and say, "*You got kicked out of heaven! You had the best of everything and you lost it. I don't want to hear any more of your yapping!*" I shared this one day with my friend, Kisha, who is a very bold and powerful woman of God, and she thought it was *so funny*. She jokingly said something to the tune of, "*I actually felt sorry for the devil for a minute; he must have thought—did you really have to go there?*" Sometimes we really need to remember that the accuser of our soul, the devil, has done abominable things over and over, so why should we listen to his accusations?

— Knowing God's Seasons and Timings —

Timing is everything! One of the key ingredients in *arising to be the powerful army of God* is that we have understanding of the times and seasons we are in. It is important to understand what God is doing on the earth so we can be in agreement with Him and be part of the solution. In 1 Chronicles 12:32, we read that the sons of Issachar had understanding of the times to know what Israel ought to do. It is important that we the people of God also have understanding of the times so that we don't miss our time of visitation.

> *Now as He drew near, He saw the city and wept over it, saying, "If you had known, even you, especially in this your day, the things that make for your peace! But now they are hidden from your eyes. For days will come upon you when your enemies will build an embankment around you, surround you and close you in on every side, and level you, and your children within you, to the ground; and they will not leave in you one stone upon another, because you **did not know the time of your visitation**.* (emphasis added)
>
> Luke 19:41–44

Many in Israel did not recognize their Messiah when He came, therefore taking them out of God's protection and blessing. History repeats itself, and sometimes, when God sends a deliverer or a move of God to bless us, we miss the blessing God sent because it didn't look like we expected.

My family and I have enjoyed reading about revival and reformation movements of the past. I especially love the story of Martin Luther, who sparked a major reformation in the

Church in the 1500s, when he nailed the ninety-five theses to the church door questioning some of the unbiblical practices they had adhered to. We celebrate him as a reformer who brought back valuable truths of the gospel of grace that had been stolen from the corporate church at that time. Though he is widely celebrated and honored today as a great Christian Reformer, the Church at that time persecuted him. Isn't that true with most moves of God? Even though many in the Church world celebrate the past revivals of God *now*, a big part of the Church at that time would miss the visitation God was bringing and actually persecute it.

Therefore, it is not uncommon for those involved in past revivals to persecute or not understand the current revival. Why is this? Probably because the new revival does not look the same as the old. However, God does not usually do the same thing the same way; He is a very creative God. It is always important, of course, that we use discernment, praying and testing the spirits (1 John 4:1) of any new move of God, but we shouldn't automatically dismiss it, either, just because it looks different.

At this time in history, we see God's hand moving in a governmental reformation which involves exposing and removing corruption at political levels. At the same time, we see God doing this same thing in the Church world to deal with any corruption there along with any changes that need to take place. Reformation is messy because it involves a clashing of good and evil as God deals with the darkness in these situations.

Our current season in our nation and around the world is *a time of war.* At this time, there are physical wars in some places, but the war I'm emphasizing is the *spiritual and ideological war* taking place. There are those who have an antichrist agenda that have waged war against the principles of God. They would love to silence our voices and take away our freedom. However, God is doing the opposite: He is planning an overthrow of the wicked corruption that has been going on for years and making room to promote His people to positions of great authority. This is not a time to be asleep and apathetic. This is time to engage in prayer and be alert to what part each one of us plays in this battle.

This reminds me of a series of articles I read a few years ago concerning a dream that Rick Joyner from Morningstar Ministries had concerning the current war we are in. The dream he had was about America being in a "Second Revolution/Civil War" that would be necessary for us to move forward. In the dream, God was handing out assignments of the parts each of us would play in this war. I don't believe this war was necessarily physical; it most likely represented the cultural and spiritual war we are currently in. I do know that he has since written a book concerning his dream titled, *The Second American Revolution/Civil War*.[2]

We didn't ask for this turbulent season we have found ourselves in, but if we look into the heart of God, we will see that victory lies on the other side of the battle, for the United States of America and for the world. We will see manifestations of God's glory that history will tell about for years to come. This is our moment. This is our hour. The curtains have been pulled back and we are taking our place in a drama between good and evil. This drama is not fiction; it is very real. Let's not miss the hour of our visitation. The battle may be hard, but the victory is going to far exceed our expectations!

For the rest of this chapter, I am going to highlight a story in the Bible where God brought forth a mighty army as an example of what God wants to do for us. This army, Gideon and the three hundred (Judges 6–8), needed a resurrection in their mind and spirit. They were alive on the outside, but dead in their confidence and vision of who they were.

The Arising of Gideon's Army

The story of Gideon and his army of only three hundred shows the miraculous favor of God when against all odds they defeated thousands of enemies. As we reflect on the story of Gideon in this chapter, I want to point out some of the similarities to the battles we are facing currently in America and around the world.

The story of Gideon is one of those least likely hero stories. This story begins with the children of Israel being oppressed by enemies that were devouring their food and leaving them hiding in dens, caves, and strongholds in the mountains. It left them impoverished, fearful, and in survival mode.

> *Then the children of Israel did evil in the sight of the Lord. So the Lord delivered them into the hand of Midian for seven years, and the hand of Midian prevailed against Israel. Because of the Midianites, the children of Israel made for themselves the dens, the caves, and the strongholds which are in the mountains. So it was, whenever Israel had sown, Midianites would come up; also Amalekites and the people of the East would come up against them. Then they would encamp against them and destroy the produce of the earth as far as Gaza, and leave no sustenance for Israel, neither sheep nor ox nor donkey. For they would come up with their livestock and their tents, coming in as numerous as locusts; both they and their camels were without number; and they would enter the land to destroy it. So Israel was greatly impoverished because of the*

> *Midianites, and the children of Israel cried out to the Lord.*
>
> Judges 6:1–6

It is a sad place to be when the people of God are hiding **IN** the mountains instead of **ON TOP** of the mountains! (I will also talk more about "taking mountains" in chapter 10.) Too often we forget that we are the head and not the tail. Too often compromise has opened the door to trouble, and we have to suffer for far too long before we "cry out to the Lord." But God is so good. All He needs is for us to cry out to Him and He will come running to our rescue! However, part of the rescue is reminding us of who we are in Him!

I find it interesting that in Judges 6:5, the Bible describes their enemies as being "as numerous as locusts." This reminds me of Joel 2:25, *"So I will restore to you the years that the swarming locust has eaten, the crawling locust, the consuming locust, and the chewing locust, My great army which I sent among you."* I have always felt that the fact that four different types of locusts are mentioned in this verse can represent to us that no matter how we got robbed and defeated, whether it was our fault or circumstances beyond our control, God always has a restoration plan when we come to Him!

The name "Gideon" means: *he that bruises or breaks, a destroyer.*[3] When we belong to Jesus, God has already placed inside of us a *breaker anointing*. Here are a few scriptures to confirm that:

> *You are of God, little children, and have overcome them, because He who is in you is greater than he who is in the world.*
>
> 1 John 4:4

> *...And the yoke will be destroyed because of the anointing oil.*
>
> Isaiah 10:27
>
> *Assuredly, I say to you, whatever you bind on earth will be bound in heaven, and whatever you loose on earth will be loosed in heaven.*
>
> Matthew 18:18

In the story of Gideon, God had already given His covenant people authority and power over their enemies; it was *their* promised land given to them from God, and they should have been ruling their land with God. However, because of their foolishness and compromise with idolatry, God allowed a chastening from their enemies, the Midianites and the Amalekites (Judges 6:1). Sometimes this is God's way of waking up His people when they have fallen away from Him, but in God's mercy and goodness, He is ready and willing to give them a plan of deliverance.

In our country, the United States of America, we have seen unprecedented corruption (that we call "deep state") in our government. This can also be a type of Midianites and the Amalekites for us since this corruption has been slowly stealing our freedoms, our wealth, and our quality of life. We are finding out now that there have been problems for a long time, but most of us didn't realize it was that bad until President Trump announced he planned to drain the swamp. Then the battle began, and we found that we had no idea how many swamp creatures had been hiding underneath those murky waters.

── Midian: Flood of Judgement, False Coverings, and Bad Habits ──

I thought it was interesting and noteworthy that the meaning of the name "Midian"[4] is *judgment; covering; habit*.

The first meaning of Midian, *judgment*, is very familiar to us right now. We have currently been in a long, uncomfortable season where there has been a lot of judgment, intimidation, and shame coming at us. Political correctness has chased us into hiding places because we don't want to upset the social media police. We see media giants take people's platforms and businesses down just because they don't share their liberal ideology. (We thought we were supposed to have freedom of speech???) We have been afraid of being falsely accused, because that lying spirit of accusation has been rampant. Remember that the devil is an accuser, and he uses people to make false accusations to put us in fear and to silence us. An example of this kind of accusation is given to us in the scripture below:

> *So the serpent spewed water out of his mouth like a flood after the woman, that he might cause her to be carried away by the flood. But the earth helped the woman, and the earth opened its mouth and swallowed up the flood which the dragon had spewed out of his mouth.*
>
> Revelation 12:15–16

It is interesting that the serpent spewed water out of his *mouth* like a flood. I believe "mouth" would represent "words." Since the first mention of "flood" in the Bible was during the time of Noah when God flooded the earth because of evil, we can assume that a flood can represent *judgment*.

Therefore, in this passage we read that the devil sends a flood of judgment against the *woman*, which I believe can be symbolic of the Church. The Church in the Bible is referred to as female since we are also called, "the Bride of Christ."

I don't think in my lifetime I have ever seen so much harsh judgment released in our nation in the form of accusations. We are followed around on social media being "fact checked" on whether our posts meet the "woke" standard. The cancel culture is the punishment meted out if you say or do what is politically incorrect. The cancel culture will get you kicked out of the social media synagogue. Your business, online platform, and reputation can be canceled very quickly. There is very little grace in this kind of society. There are people just waiting to catch someone in their words. By the way, that is what the Pharisees did to Jesus: they watched His words to see if they could catch Him in anything! Having your words watched is *not very much fun to say the least!*

Judgment can cause us to run and hide. It can silence us, which is the enemy's goal. This is the case in the time of Gideon. The people just got used to being robbed and silenced, so they were in hiding. They had gotten comfortable with their abusers. They had stopped believing for a change.

My friend and mentor of many years, Judy Taylor, taught me as a young Christian a principle that I see lived out again and again. She said, *"The accuser is guilty of what they accuse!"* A scriptural reference for this can be found in Romans 2:1, *"Therefore you are inexcusable, O man, whoever you are who judge, for in whatever you judge another you condemn yourself; for you who judge practice the same things."* I have seen that be true so many times when someone falsely accuses me or someone else, that down the road you will notice that they were doing what they accused you or someone else of and *usually worse*. (I'm not talking about when someone has actual facts that they need to confront someone with; I'm speaking of the attitude of false accusation when the person *knows* they are lying about somebody.)

The second meaning of the name Midian is *covering*. When I think of the word "covering," I think of protection. Psalms 91 is a psalm in which God promises to be that covering and protection to us. In Psalms 91:4, we read, *"He shall cover you with His feathers, and under His wings you shall take refuge."* Parents who love and want what's best for their children are examples of the proper kind of covering and protection. When the heart of any kind of leader, whether in government, workplace, or any place in society, is in line with the heart of God, then their desire should be to care for, love, and protect.

However, many of us have been shocked as we realize that many of our leaders have not had our best interest in mind. We have a media that lies shamelessly over and over just to protect their favorite people. We have found out that many politicians have lied and deceived just to keep their positions and benefits. A real leader does the right thing even when it is not in their best interest.

Lucifer is an example of a bad covering or authority figure. In Ezekiel 28:16, Lucifer is referred to as a *"covering cherub."* Whoa, that is a true example of bad authority! The devil not only defiled himself and got kicked out of heaven, but he took a third of the angels down with him. Examples of bad coverings or authority figures are ones who control for their own gain and don't care about the people under them. In John 10:10–16, Jesus teaches us the difference between a good shepherd who cares about the sheep and the hireling that does not protect and leaves the sheep vulnerable to enemies.

It is not hard to look at examples in all areas of society and see the difference between true leaders who do what is right even if it is not popular versus the ones who are in it for themselves and merely use people to get what they want. In politics, we see many examples of career politicians that will do whatever is necessary to stay in power and have no concern of what is really best for the people they represent. Unfortunately, sometimes church leaders can also become so concerned with what is best for the *success* of their ministry, that they lose sight of the needs of the people God has entrusted them with. Jesus gave us the true definition of leadership: the greatest will serve (Matthew 23:11).

The third meaning of the name Midian is *habit*. Habits can make or break you. Good habits like spending time with God and reading your Bible make a huge difference in your quality of life. Bad habits like addictions and wrong thinking patterns can bring you to a place of defeat. Allowing others to repeatedly take advantage of you can also be considered a bad habit. The problem in the story of Gideon was that the enemies had a *habit* of stealing their harvest and their things, and Israel had just gotten used to it. Remember that our enemy, the devil, comes to *steal, kill, and destroy* (John 10:10). However, in the same passage we read that Jesus came to give us *abundant life*. Therefore, it is not God's desire for us to put up in any way with the devil stealing our abundant life! This is a time for the people of God to wake up, not just to what is happening in the world around us, but also in our personal lives.

This reminds me of Disney/Pixar's movie, *A Bug's Life*. The ants would do all the work, and then the grasshoppers would fly in and take their food. When the main character of the movie, Flik, tried to challenge what had become the norm, he initially got persecuted by the other ants who didn't want to upset the nasty, intimidating grasshoppers. Sound familiar?

Abuse can happen anywhere, whether it is in large groups of people or just in your own personal lives. Whenever any kind of abuse goes on long enough, it can lull us to sleep, and we can get to a place where the abuse becomes "normalized." We get in trouble when we allow people to abuse, control, and take advantage of us. Most of us Christians are peace-loving people who really don't want to get in a tussle. However, compromising to avoid the fight is only going to give us *fake peace, not true peace.*

One of the other bad habits that Israel had gotten into was idolatry. In Judges 6:25, God calls Gideon to tear down the altar of Baal. Baal was a false god that many in Israel were worshiping at that time. The worship of Baal sometimes included ritual prostitution and child-sacrifice.[5] Today, this can represent sexual immoralities in our culture along with the practice of abortion. Abortion in our society has been one of those Baal worshiping idols that we the Church have been praying and believing to be removed. Thankfully, on June 24th, 2022, the United States Supreme Court overturned "Roe v. Wade," taking away abortion rights on a federal level. That was a great victory for righteousness; however, we are still praying for abortion to also be overturned on state and local levels.

Idolatry can represent anything that our society worships instead of the one true God. Gideon apparently knew he was going to upset some people by tearing down the altar of Baal. In fact, he was so scared that he did it by night! (Sounds like Nicodemus in John 3:2. He came to Jesus *by night*, most likely not to upset his Pharisee friends!) However, Gideon obeyed, so we will give him credit for that! Joyce Meyer often tells us in her sermons to "do it afraid"—it still counts![6] And yes, he stirred up demonic warfare. The people were upset that their idol was torn down.

This is true for us today. Sometimes God calls us to make a stand and speak truth against something in society or even among close friends and family that we know is wrong. That can be scary because we know we might get a huge backlash when we tear down idols, especially the popular ones! We might get unfriended by a lot of people. However, we must remember that just like Gideon, God is with us, and He will fight our battles.

Amalek: A People Who Licks Up

The name "Amalek"[7] means *"a people that licks up."* That sounds to me like **devouring**. It reminds me of the COVID-19 virus and the destruction it has caused. It sounds like a takeover. It reminds me of rioting in cities and takeovers on our social media. The liberal agenda has definitely been in a takeover mode. They have been riding on the top of the media mountain, education mountain, political mountain, and most of the other mountains also, which we will talk about in a later chapter. They have been telling us what it is okay to say and think. It has bled over into so many areas of society, it is too numerous to list. Wherever it is, it has not been pleasant.

One of the ways the enemy has been attacking today is through "fake news." They believe that repeating the same lies to us over and over again will cement it in our minds and brainwash us. Ask God to help you choose right news sources that are honest and have actual facts to back up their claims. Since faith comes by hearing (Romans 10:17), then we must know that the opposite happens when we listen to the wrong voices: fear and deception.

An example of a scripture that describes devouring is 1 Peter 5:8, *"Be sober, be vigilant; because your adversary the devil walks about like a roaring lion, seeking whom he may devour."* One way the enemy devours is by stealing our confidence with thoughts of inadequacy: he roars accusations at our minds. Other ways he devours are by actually stealing from us financially or physically, or attacking our quality of life. Notice, the scripture above says that the enemy seeks *whom he may devour.* That means that we have the choice of whether we put up with it or not.

In the time of Gideon, the enemies were devouring all their food and wealth. As I previously pointed out in chapter one, one of the movements we have been fighting against in the world today is a rise of socialist and communist agendas.

Many of us Americans that have been alive for some time never would have thought that we would even be seriously considering this type of government. In countries where these systems operate, people are left in poverty with only the people on top having the wealth. These systems tend to eliminate the middle class. People are left hungry and hopeless with no viable pathway to a better life. This is what the enemy wants to do in America and around the world. This is a form of devouring, like the Amalek spirit. This is an example of what Jesus told us that the enemy does—coming to kill, steal, and destroy.

This is a promise that applies to us from the prophet, Isaiah:

> *The Lord has sworn by His right hand*
> *and by the arm of His strength:*
> *"Surely I will no longer give your grain*
> *as food for your enemies;*
> *And the sons of the foreigner shall not drink*
> *your new wine,*
> *for which you have labored.*
> *But those who have gathered it shall eat it,*
> *and praise the Lord;*
> *Those who have brought it together shall*
> *drink it in My holy courts."*
> Isaiah 62:8–9

—— Removing Our Excuses and Unbelief ——

In the following passage, we read how God called Gideon to go fight the Midianites, yet Gideon responded to God with excuses of why he was not the right one for the job!

> *Now the Angel of the Lord came and sat under the terebinth tree which was in Ophrah, which belonged to Joash the Abiezrite, while his son Gideon threshed wheat in the winepress, in order to hide it from the Midianites. And the Angel of the Lord appeared to him, and said to him, "**The Lord is with you, you mighty man of valor**!"*
>
> *Gideon said to Him, "O my lord, if the Lord is with us, why then has all this happened to us? And where are all His miracles which our fathers told us about, saying, 'Did not the Lord bring us up from Egypt?' But now the Lord has forsaken us and delivered us into the hands of the Midianites."*
>
> *Then the Lord turned to him and said, "Go in this **might** of yours, and you shall save Israel from the hand of the Midianites. Have I not sent you?"*
>
> *So he said to Him, "O my Lord, how can I save Israel? Indeed my clan is the weakest in Manasseh, and I am the least in my father's house."*
>
> *And the Lord said to him, "Surely I will be with you, and you shall defeat the Midianites as one man."* (emphasis added)
>
> Judges 6:11–16

Let's look at Gideon's excuses and how God responded:

Gideon found it hard to believe that the Lord was with them when bad things were happening. God responds to Gideon by telling him his assignment as a deliverer! How many times do we hear those kinds of responses from the world—well, if God is real, then why do bad things happen? The truth of the matter is that God partners with His people over the earth. Until God puts away the enemy for good, He will partner with us in battle, promising to be with us. In Israel's case they were compromising with false gods, and compromise opens the door for their enemies. However, in God's mercy and love, He comes up with a plan for their deliverance.

Gideon tells God that his clan was the weakest in Manasseh, and he was the least in his father's house. God again ignores his excuse and gives Gideon a mighty promise that He will be with him and give him victory over their enemies. In 1 Corinthians 1:27 it says, *"But God has chosen the foolish things of the world to put to shame the wise, and God has chosen the weak things of the world to put to shame the things which are mighty."* Remember that God loves to exalt the humble and those who feel inadequate because He wants our confidence to be in Him. The prideful don't usually get God's promotions because God wants us to come to Him as little children (Matthew 18:3).

Gideon's excuses remind me of the story of the twelve men of Israel sent to spy out the promised land in Numbers 13. We read that only two of them, Caleb and Joshua, came back agreeing with God that they could take the land. The other ten brought their excuses:

> *And they gave the children of Israel a bad report of the land which they had spied out, saying, "The land through which we have gone as spies is a land that devours its inhabitants, and all the people whom we saw in it are men of great stature. There we saw the giants (the descendants of Anak came from the*

> *giants); and we were like grasshoppers in our own sight, and so we were in their sight."*
>
> Numbers 13:32–33

Just like God didn't pay any attention to Gideon's excuses, God did not accept the ten negative spies' report either. In fact, in the story of the twelve spies, only Caleb and Joshua pleased God and were allowed to enter the promised land. The rest of Israel had to wander in the wilderness for forty years until the faithless generation had died out.

How does this relate to us? Well, we know that we have been in a war over our country's, the United States of America's, Christian and moral values. Much of the same battle is happening in other parts of the world. The Midianites (social media police and political Pharisees) and the Amalekites (fake news and socialism agenda) are robbing our country and us of our liberty and resources. This is an hour where we need to continue to partner with God in prayer and be willing to take this land back for God. (I do not mean a physical war here, I'm talking about a spiritual war that is won in prayer and by using our voices—not allowing our freedom of speech to be violated.)

The Remnant of 300

God always wants us to keep our eyes on Him and how powerful He is, and not focus on ourselves. The currency of heaven is faith and God delights that we trust Him when He gives us an assignment. God is never going to tell us to do something and not back us up with His power.

God calls those things that are not as though they are (Romans 4:17). The very fact *God* called Gideon "mighty" caused him to become "mighty"! God has creative power when He speaks over us. He called Abraham a father of many nations before he had any children (Genesis 17:5). When God speaks something over you, He causes you to become that! The very fact that He promises to be with us and never leave us lets us know that we can have assurance of victory. Since we are made in the image of God, we should just speak over ourselves what we know God says about us. We can do this by making declarations that are promised to us in the Bible. We can also do this by reminding and speaking over ourselves personal promises God has said to us in prayer or by prophecies from others. This will build our faith and make it strong against the lies of the enemy!

In Judges 6:16, God says to Gideon that he shall defeat the Midianites as one man! Well, Gideon actually had three hundred men at the end of the testing of the troops; however, since three hundred might as well have been just one in comparison to the multiplied thousands that the enemy had, God is saying 'I am the one doing the fighting for you, so trust Me!' God loves to use a small remnant of people to do something mighty because… If God be for you, who can be against you?

In Judges 7:4–6, the Lord tested the people in order to get the army down to the serious ones. First, you see the group go home who were fearful. Now let me make a comment here that the fearful here *chose fear*—they chose to not believe and trust God. It doesn't mean that you had to go home if you *felt* fear as an emotion. Probably everyone there had some level of feeling fear; after all, they were about to go to war! But the point is that no matter what we are feeling, we need to say *yes* to God and trust that He will work out the details. Secondly, you had the next round of testing on the remainder of the troops who went to drink water, which was based on *how* they drank. God told Gideon to separate out the ones who got on their knees to drink from the ones who lapped (brought the water up in their hands to drink). God chose the ones (three hundred) who brought the water up with their hands. You see that this group was prepared for war, because they were aware of their surroundings while they drank. They discerned the times and seasons they were in. They were drinking from the Lord but also staying in warrior mode to discern what was going on around them.

Even though God would love for as many of His people to be involved in His cause as possible, He can save by few or many (1 Samuel 14:6). Many times it is a small remnant that is used to turn things around, not necessarily the multitudes.

We can apply this principle to our personal lives and in our current cultural war in America and around the world. Like the sons of Issachar (1 Chronicles 12:32), God wants us to discern the times and seasons we are in. The three hundred in this story understood that the liberty of their nation was at stake. They discerned what fake news was, who was lying and who was telling the truth. They discerned who the anointing was on for leadership and who was only there for their own gain.

The famous slogan that President Donald Trump has always campaigned on, "Make America Great Again," is an example of the mindset that we should have. (As I'm writing this, Donald Trump is not in the White House because of a stolen election. However, he won and I believe he will be restored!) Donald Trump does not believe it is okay to ignore problems like our economy, our border security, or unfair trade deals, along with many other issues. What decades of politicians have ignored and just got used to, he believed we could and should fix! In the midst of chaos, great national debt, and huge political division, he still believes in the greatness of America and the American people. That is what God does when He calls those things that are not as though they are; he causes the greatness and destiny that He has already put inside of us to arise and be seen.

In the story of Gideon, I believe that Israel had allowed their enemies to steal from them because they did not believe that "God was with them." They didn't believe they were mighty. They didn't believe they had a voice. They didn't believe if they prayed God would work a miracle for them. We are also not sure how long Israel had compromised with idolatry which led to their defeat at the hands of their enemies. It was most likely not just one particular day of idolatry, but an increase of their sin over a span of time. It was not just one day that we have become in trouble in America either. It has been decades of compromise, but God wants to bring about a mighty reformation. I believe that God wants to make our country great again, and we need to agree with Him!

We need to remember that whether we got ourselves into the mess, or someone else has imposed it on us, we need to realize that God will always provide a way of escape. Just like Gideon was given a specific plan from God, we must also ask God to give us direction in any place where we need deliverance.

> *No temptation has overtaken you except such as is common to man; but God is faithful, who will not allow you to be tempted beyond what you are able, but with the temptation will also make the* **way of escape**, *that you may be able to bear it.* (emphasis added)
>
> 1 Corinthians 10:13

── Receiving Confirmation and Encouragement ──

The story goes on with Gideon asking God to give him some confirmations. God patiently gave it to him every time he asked. God is okay with you wanting to be sure about something before you do it. He will give you the confirmations you need! God says in the multitude of counsel, there is safety (Proverbs 11:14). Therefore, it is good to pray with trusted friends and leaders and ask God for confirmations in situations, but after you have had some reliable confirmations, just step out and believe God is with you! We don't want to be like the children of Israel, who were deaf and blind to the prophets that were rising up and speaking daily. We need to trust that we are His sheep and if we ask Him to speak to us, He promises to do so! (Jeremiah 33:3, John 10:27)

In America, we have had much prophetic encouragement from many leaders in the Body of Christ that God wants to heal our land and deliver us from demonic forces. I'm sure you have had your own times with the Lord during which He has spoken encouragement to you also; I know I have had many of those times with the Lord. Sometimes God will even give you encouragement from your enemies:

> *And when Gideon had come, there was a man telling a dream to his companion. He said, "I have had a dream: To my surprise, a loaf of barley bread tumbled into the camp of Midian; it came to a tent and struck it so that it fell and overturned, and the tent collapsed."*
>
> *Then his companion answered and said, "This is nothing else but the sword of Gideon*

> *the son of Joash, a man of Israel! Into his hand God has delivered Midian and the whole camp."*
>
> Judges 7:13–14

The enemy is more afraid of us than we realize. The enemy knows that God is on our side. They have heard how the Lord has defeated our enemies in the past. Rahab said that the people of Jericho had been afraid of Israel for forty years ever since they heard what happened to Pharaoh's army at the Red Sea (Joshua 2:9–11). It is time for the people of God to know **who we are**, and it doesn't matter if our enemies outnumber us because our victory comes from the Lord!

For example, when we see the devil really nervous about something, it is usually because God is up to something really good! We are not usually aware of the light and anointing on us that the enemy sees. Many times, we have allowed the enemy to steal our confidence by seeing ourselves as grasshoppers and our enemies as giants, but God sees the opposite. We are the ones with His power and authority!

Another interesting note in Judges 7:13–14 highlighted above is the fact that in the enemy's dream of defeat, a loaf of *barley bread* tumbled into their camp representing Gideon. As I studied the history of barley bread[5] in the Bible, I found it interesting that barley bread was used by the poorer people of the land. I think this again is a type and shadow of God using the least likely and weakest to pour out His power on. That should make us all feel included!

> *And so it was, when Gideon heard the telling of the dream and its interpretation, that he worshiped. He returned to the camp of Israel, and said, "Arise, for the Lord has delivered the camp of Midian into your*

hand." Then he divided the three hundred men into three companies, and he put a trumpet into every man's hand, with empty pitchers, and torches inside the pitchers. And he said to them, "Look at me and do likewise; watch, and when I come to the edge of the camp you shall do as I do: When I blow the trumpet, I and all who are with me, then you also blow the trumpets on every side of the whole camp, and say, 'The sword of the Lord and of Gideon!'"

So Gideon and the hundred men who were with him came to the outpost of the camp at the beginning of the middle watch, just as they had posted the watch; and they blew the trumpets and broke the pitchers that were in their hands. Then the three companies blew the trumpets and broke the pitchers—they held the torches in their left hands and the trumpets in their right hands for blowing— and they cried, "The sword of the Lord and of Gideon!" And every man stood in his place all around the camp; and the whole army ran and cried out and fled. When the three hundred blew the trumpets, the Lord set every man's sword against his companion throughout the whole camp; and the army fled to Beth Acacia, toward Zererah, as far as the border of Abel Meholah, by Tabbath.

Judges 7:15–22

It is significant prophetically for the Church in America to recognize that the enemy was defeated with a trumpet and a lantern. I believe that the trumpet is prophetic for our country because of President Donald Trump, who has been a trumpet to alert us and point out the deep swamp in our own country and other worldly enemies we have been fighting. (We are also trumpets for the Lord when we use our voices to speak truth, pray, and make declarations.) The lantern would represent the Church who is full of light and the oil of the Holy Spirit. We have been praying and prophesying the exposure of our enemies. Jesus also called His people the "light of the world" in Matthew 5:14.

It is also significant that the enemies were destroying each other in the story of Gideon. They first turned their swords on each other, and then Israel chased down the rest of them. This reminds me of the story of Jehoshaphat in 2 Chronicles 20. In this story, the army began to praise and worship, and the enemies killed one another. They didn't have to fight at all. In fact, *every* enemy was defeated! When we follow God's plan, our victories are easy!

People who walk in darkness often turn on each other, because their alliances are not based on love and respect. They join forces not based on the right reasons, but on their need to get what they want. However, if anything starts going wrong, like people getting caught doing things, they will turn on each other in a nanosecond! I totally believe we will see this in our American swamp.

—— You Are Mighty

You may not feel mighty, but you are because of what Jesus did for us at the cross. If you have invited Jesus to be your Lord and Savior, then you are mighty. If you were born again just five minutes ago, you can send demons packing (shrieking and crying like babies) with just one word: "Jesus." On our worst days, we are still mighty because Jesus lives on the inside of us and He is ALWAYS MIGHTY. The devil DOES NOT want us to know we are mighty. He is afraid that if we knew that—if we *really* knew that—we might use our weapons against Him. Then he would not get away with all the stealing, killing, and destroying.

This battle requires all hands on deck! I want everyone who reads this book to know that every one of us is "mighty in God." We each have untapped potential that we don't know of. God has put special gifts on the inside of each of us that no one else has. We are all so valuable and irreplaceable to Father God. We each have different thumbprints because we are all unique and different. Together we are a mighty army!

There is something awesome when the mighty arise. It is like the United States Army after the bombing of Pearl Harbor. Men were packing their bags and running to the enlistment offices. They were kissing their families goodbye, not knowing if they would return or not. It was called patriotism: love of God and country. It was the kind of patriotism that King David had the first time he heard the sound of Goliath mocking their country, Israel, and mocking their God. He was like—what??—who is this uncircumcised Philistine that dares to insult us and our God like that (1 Samuel 17:26)? Patriotism is arising in our nation right now and our enemies will most likely wish they had not *woken* us up. This is not to be confused with *liberal* "wokeness." This kind of "awakening" is because we have realized that our liberties are being stolen and we want them back!

You first have to awaken yourself. Awaken yourself to the mighty warrior that is inside of you. Then awaken those around you in your family, community, and churches. Little awakenings lead to big awakenings, and pretty soon, our nation will be shaken back awake with a move of the Spirit of God and patriotism again!

The Church can be likened to a sleeping giant. Many times we don't even realize we are asleep until the enemy starts picking on us. I believe God is awakening His Church right now to the reality of how powerful we really are. God is preparing us as an army. This is a time for war (Ecclesiastes 3:8). We will get the time of peace after the time of war, as in the order of that scripture. The war is messy but worth it. We can suffer now or suffer later…

Closing Remarks

In closing, most of us, if we are honest, resonate with Gideon. Whether it be dreams in our personal lives or our dream of a better America, we sometimes lack the confidence needed to move forward in those dreams. Remember, God doesn't usually give you a dream when you already have it all together; then you might be tempted to be proud! And we have read the Bible and know what happens to the proud. God doesn't want us to end up being a Saul (1 Samuel 15:17–19)! Many times He takes us through a LONG process, much longer than we would have guessed. If you have been through a long process, be encouraged and know that it is a compliment from God. My dear friend Judy once told me when you see people sprout up with amazing anointings seemingly overnight, that is not always a compliment. God knows that some people are going to need some quick results in order to stay with Him and would not be able to handle the long process. Therefore, if your process has been long, be encouraged and believe that God is developing and fine-tuning the mighty warrior inside of you!

You may feel like you have been hidden; Gideon was one of the hidden ones. Gideon would not have been the one picked by his country to be the new leader of God's army. He wouldn't even have picked himself. But God picked him, and this is going to be a season of God picking the most unlikely people. God pulled him out of obscurity and made history with him. This will be a time for the hidden ones to arise. Don't disqualify yourself because of your family name or your public platform, or your wealth, degrees, etc. God has chosen you. He loves to choose the weak and foolish things of this world to confound the mighty.

Also, if you think you are too old, talk to Abraham and Sarah. We can be timeless with the Lord. He can renew our youth. (I am seriously standing on the youth renewal promises!) Think outside of the box into the impossible. Don't think natural: 'I only have this many years left.' Decide you are going to believe that you live outside of time with God, which we do because we are seated with Him in heavenly places. We are not natural; we are supernatural because of God living on the inside of us.

In the next chapter, we are going to discuss another army that needed to arise. This army, however, would not just need a spiritual resurrection like Gideon's three hundred; this one would need a *physical* resurrection!

CAN THESE BONES LIVE?
The Resurrection of America
Chapter 3

> *The hand of the Lord came upon me and brought me out in the Spirit of the Lord, and set me down in the midst of the valley; and it was full of bones. Then He caused me to pass by them all around, and behold, there were very many in the open valley; and indeed they were very dry. And He said to me, "Son of man, **can these bones live**?" So I answered, "O Lord God, You know."* (emphasis added)
>
> Ezekiel 37:1–3

A Stretch of Faith

Bones! Imagine with me for a moment being the great prophet, Ezekiel. The Lord takes you in the Spirit and sits you down in the middle of a valley full of bones. Notice the valley is **full** of bones, not just a few. And if it wasn't enough just to sit there and get a big overview of what this death valley looks like, God then takes it to the next level and has you pass by these bones all around (probably very slowly) to make sure you see the full picture and all the details! As you get a close-up view, you comprehend that the bones are dry, and not just dry, but VERY DRY. No life to these bones whatsoever and probably not for many years. Now when you are still wondering what God is about to reveal to you, what great revelation He is about to expound to you, instead He asks YOU a question, *"Son of man, can these bones live?"* In your mind you are saying, "I see no signs of life at all! These bones are so old and so dry that they have cracked and fallen into pieces!" However, not wanting to answer God with a lack of faith or, worse yet, sarcasm, you manage to say respectfully, *"O Lord God, you know!"*

This story was real life for the prophet Ezekiel. We cannot know for sure what he was thinking, but we can certainly imagine that his faith was being stretched by what God asked him to do. However, the beautiful part of this is that in every story in the Bible, God is building faith for all of us that nothing is impossible when we partner with God. This story is an amazing illustration that we, like Ezekiel, can prophesy to the impossible and believe for resurrection in any situation.

This story has been one of my favorite stories for most of my Christian life! I loved it when I heard sermons on this. It always infused faith in me that if God could do it once, He could certainly do it again and again. Several years ago, as I was praying to see revival in this nation and having great concern that our Christian values were eroding, God gave me this story as an example of how to pray for this nation. When you really meditate on this story and the gravity of how dead these bones were, then we can know that no matter how bad anything looks, or how long it has gone on, God can bring life and resurrection.

Can America's Destiny Live?

The question in Ezekiel 37:3, *"... Son of man, can these bones live?"* is a question that many are asking when it comes to the Christian and moral values of our nation, the United States of America. Some have questioned whether or not our current constitutional values will survive this battle—whether or not we will continue to enjoy our current religious liberties and freedom of speech. We have been dismayed by a media that is no longer interested in publishing truth, but instead would rather push a left-wing agenda like propaganda and persecute those who oppose this kind of thought pattern. They have become disrespectful to those of us of faith, mocking our values and accusing us falsely. The sanctity of our nation has been challenged. It has all been quite shocking, to say the least.

Not only are we asking, *"Can these bones live?"*, but we are asking if each part can be put back in their rightful positions. In order for those bones lying in a field to live, they will have to be connected in the right place in unity in order for life to be put back into them. Because otherwise, it may look a bit scary—an arm over here, a head over there…well, you get the picture.

Despite what we see in the natural, we need to look higher to our God, because He is speaking to us with hope and promises of a much better future, but God needs us to be in agreement and alignment with Him. He wants to partner with His Church in America, and I believe we will see great reformation and revival because no matter how bad it looks, our God is always bigger and more powerful! We need to look to Jesus, the author and finisher of our faith, the author and finisher of this nation, and believe that all things are possible. Could we the Church in America believe that God could resurrect those dry and dead Christian values and foundations in our country? I knew the answer God wanted us to say was YES! We know that in God all His promises are Yes and Amen (I Corinthians 1:20).

Back to the story of the dry bones, Ezekiel said that the bones were VERY DRY! In other words, they had been dead for a long time! Have you ever noticed that many times, God rescues when the situation is most dire? The Red Sea is a good example of this. The children of Israel stuck between an ocean and a mighty army could definitely be described by the expression 'stuck between a rock and a hard place'! The stories of Daniel being thrown in the lion's den (Daniel 6) and his three friends being thrown in the fiery furnace (Daniel 3) are both examples of last minute rescues. I'm sure Daniel and his three friends would rather have had the rescue come *before* they were thrown into these places. Even Joseph in his plight of being sold into slavery saw his situation go from bad to worse when he ended up in prison on false charges. However, the drama of these stories are not only testimonies of God's faithfulness to us; they are testimonies to the kings and people of their times who witnessed these dramatic interventions of God.

The good news in all of these stories is that in the language of God, which is a language of faith, He is letting us know that there is NOTHING impossible with Him, no matter how bad things look! Therefore, we can certainly believe for great victory and restoration in our nation. God has a wonderful plan for us and our best days are ahead. I believe God wants to partner with His people, the Body of Christ, to see a miraculous reformation!

In the story of the dry bones, even though the prophet Ezekiel was prophesying over his country, Israel, I felt the power of God jump out from those scriptures, hearing it as if

God was speaking directly to the Church in America concerning our country America. Let's look at what God said to Ezekiel:

> *And He said to me, "Son of man, can these bones live?" So I answered, "O Lord God, You know."*
>
> Ezekiel 37:3

I think it is very interesting that God began by letting Ezekiel *see* the state of the bones—dry, dead, lifeless—and then He asked Ezekiel the question, *"Can these bones live?"* I thought it was very intelligent on Ezekiel's part to not speak immediately of the negativity that he saw. Ezekiel obviously didn't have a vision for the bones himself, but he was intuitive enough to figure out that God did, so he eloquently responded, *"O Lord God, You know."* It is definitely a lesson for us all to learn to keep our mouths shut when we are about to speak doom and gloom over a situation. We need to wait to speak God's message of hope. We need to speak what we want to see and believe God to resurrect and heal what is broken. Remember that it takes no faith to see the obvious, but it takes faith to see what is possible with God. When we speak the miraculous and line our words in agreement with God, things will begin to shift in our favor!

I'm reminded of when God asked the prophet Jeremiah a question:

> *Moreover the word of the Lord came to me, saying, "Jeremiah, what do you **see**?..."*
> (emphasis added)
>
> Jeremiah 1:11

Our vision is very important, because what we see in our mind, we will speak. What we speak as a Christian is powerful enough to move mountains (Matthew 17:20).

Are you seeing the ruin of a nation or do you see that God has a plan to overthrow the wicked and answer the prayers of the saints and make America great again? Has God ever **not** answered the prayers of the righteous? The Bible says the prayers of a righteous man avails much (James 5:16–18). The prayers of one man (Elijah) changed a nation. We definitely have way more than that praying in the Body of Christ. Do you see the cloud the size of a man's hand or do you see famine? Do you hear the sound of the abundance of rain or do you hear the sound of silence and hopelessness? Do you hear the sound of God's voice speaking hope? Do you hear His footsteps coming closer to bring a divine rescue? I hear Him and I see Him on His way!

Let's look at the rest of the conversation between God and Ezekiel over the dry bones and see the spiritual parallels that we can apply:

> *Again He said to me, "Prophesy to these bones, and say to them, 'O dry bones, hear the word of the Lord! Thus says the Lord God to these bones: "Surely I will cause breath to enter into you, and you shall live. I will put sinews on you and bring flesh upon you, cover you with skin and put breath in you; and you shall live. Then you shall know that I am the Lord."'*
>
> *So I prophesied as I was commanded; and as I prophesied, there was a noise, and suddenly a rattling; and the bones came together, bone to bone. Indeed, as I looked, the sinews and the flesh came upon them, and*

> *the skin covered them over; but there was no breath in them.*
>
> *Also He said to me, "Prophesy to the breath, prophesy, son of man, and say to the breath, 'Thus says the Lord God: "Come from the four winds, O breath, and breathe on these slain, that they may live."' So I prophesied as He commanded me, and breath came into them, and they lived, and stood upon their feet, an exceedingly great army.*
>
> *Then He said to me, "Son of man, these bones are the whole house of Israel. They indeed say, 'Our bones are dry, our hope is lost, and we ourselves are cut off!' Therefore prophesy and say to them, 'Thus says the Lord God: "Behold, O My people, I will open your graves and cause you to come up from your graves, and bring you into the land of Israel. Then you shall know that I am the Lord, when I have opened your graves, O My people, and brought you up from your graves. I will put My Spirit in you, and you shall live, and I will place you in your own land. Then you shall know that I, the Lord, have spoken it and performed it," says the Lord.'"*
>
> Ezekiel 37:4–14

Notice that there were steps in the above passage. God commanded Ezekiel to prophesy to the dead, lifeless bones what their future would look like. God could have said, "Ezekiel, watch Me as I raise from the dead this bunch of dead bones!" How many times do we secretly hope to just sit back quietly and watch God do something and He interrupts our thoughts with 'I want *you* to speak and prophesy over this situation!' It seems that many times when we need to speak life the most, we don't feel like it. Why? Because we are looking in the natural and feeling hopeless when we need to look past the natural and into what God is doing. The hopelessness of the situation has many times stolen our joy, and since the joy of the Lord is our strength, we don't even feel like speaking in faith—that can seem like too much work. Also, the oppression of the battle can feel overwhelming. However, God always wants to partner with us. For example, in the story of Moses when he and the children of Israel were caught between Pharaoh's army and the Red Sea, Moses cried out to the Lord and the Lord basically said: 'What are you waiting for? Stretch out your rod!' For us the rod would be using our authority in prayer and declarations:

> *And the Lord said to Moses, "Why do you cry to Me? Tell the children of Israel to go forward. But lift up your rod, and stretch our hand over the sea and divide it. And the children of Israel shall go on dry ground through the midst of the sea."*
>
> Exodus 14:15–16

The first time Ezekiel prophesied, the bones came together and were covered by flesh, but there was no life yet. Then God told Ezekiel to prophesy again, and life was breathed into them, thus becoming a great army of people. God always requires persistence to our faith! Therefore, each stage of God's resurrection of these dead bones began by having Ezekiel prophesy. There is always the element of persistence when we walk with God. God definitely partners with us. He has made us into His image and wants us to prophesy the will of God to this nation!

This reminds me of the scripture in Romans 4:17:

> *...God who gives life to the dead, and calls those things that do not exist as though they did;*

God was calling Abraham a "father of many nations" long before he had any children. Even when Abraham and Sarah made a wrong choice that resulted in Ishmael, it did not change God's plan for them to have Isaac. I think we can rest assured that even though America has definitely made some wrong choices resulting in birthing some bad circumstances for this nation, God's plan and covenant for America is still the one he originally gave to the founding fathers—one to prosper and bless us—giving us a wonderful future in Him!

God backed Ezekiel's obedience to prophesy hope over something that looked and seemed hopeless by bringing a mighty resurrection from a bunch of dry, dead bones, turning them into a vibrant, mighty army. In case Ezekiel didn't get what this was all about, God was careful to explain that this army was the house of Israel, and though they had lost their hope and had been exiled to another land, he was going to bring about a restoration and deliverance and bring them back into their own land. For us in America, that speaks to the spiritual battle over our nation, for which God plans to bring a Godly restoration and reformation and bring us back to our own land, which would equal God's original purpose and call for America. I believe the phrase "place you in your own land" will also be the maintaining of our national sovereignty and borders. As you know, our borders and national sovereignty are currently under attack, which we will discuss more in chapter seven. When God brings restoration, God always restores better than it would have been if we had not gotten into a mess! God's plan is always the best plan! For us individually, we want to come into our own land—our own promised land.

Let me just say something additional about the God kind of restoration. Some people like to argue that the original plan for America is obsolete, because the founding fathers weren't perfect and Americans had moral flaws. First of all, last I checked, the only *perfect* person EVER on this earth was our Lord Jesus Christ. All the rest of us have flaws and weaknesses. That is why God's restoration is always better than the past—because the past wasn't perfect. The founding fathers had it right when they declared liberty and justice for all, but they obviously didn't fully live that, or slavery would have never existed in America. Therefore, just because America didn't fully obey their original purpose doesn't mean God changed His mind. An example of this began in the garden when God told Adam and Eve to take dominion and be fruitful and multiply. Unfortunately, they gave their dominion to the enemy, but God's plan was always the same. God still wants His people to spiritually take dominion and be fruitful and multiply. Therefore, I believe that God has given America an anointing and mandate to demonstrate what liberty and justice looks like; I believe those words came from God, and He has not changed his mind!

Not only can these verses in Ezekiel be applied to our nation or any other nation, but I see that this can also be applied to the Body of Christ, God's Church around the world! Even though God calls us His body, we don't exactly look very much like a body right now. We look very scattered, divided, and in some places, just plain dead! Therefore, we also need to prophesy that the Body of Christ comes together in the kind of unity that would glorify God. We will discuss this more in chapter eight.

When you think of the politically charged environment we are in with such division in our nation, I find it interesting that in Ezekiel 37:15, God tells the prophet to join two sticks together to represent the two divisions in Israel becoming one.

We definitely want to believe for God to do a beautiful work of unity in our nation again and also the Church!

> *Again the word of the Lord came to me, saying, "As for you, son of man, take a stick for yourself and write on it: 'For Judah and for the children of Israel, his companions.' Then take another stick and write on it, 'For Joseph, the stick of Ephraim, and for all the house of Israel, his companions.' Then join them one to another for yourself into one stick, and they will become one in your hand."*
>
> Ezekiel 37:15–17

In my spiritual imagination, I couldn't help but see the potential of political unity in our nation! I know that is a HUGE stretch, but not any more impossible than resurrecting a bunch of dry, dead bones and turning them into a mighty army. With God, nothing is impossible. Now that kind of unity only works if everyone is on the same page with God—because God is always right! There are unfortunately many who are not standing on the side of God right now. Many of the leaders of the Democratic Party in my opinion have willingly chosen darkness—the reason why they are willing to lie, cheat, steal, and run this country off a steep cliff, just as long as they stay in power. Also, there is no way that the killing of the unborn can be justified in the eyes of God. Even though many of us thought the Republican Party have been more on God's agenda, we have seen the swamp emerge there also. I do believe that many political leaders are in the valley of decision right now and unless they submit to God, their lampstand will be removed (Revelation 2:5), and God will replace their positions with people willing to serve God and the people of this country.

Resurrections

This whole idea of "resurrections" from the story of the Dry Bones in Ezekiel 37 was one of the first ingredients of this book that God showed me. One beautiful confirmation God gave me that I was on the right track was in the fall of 2018. My husband and I had attended a Christian conference, and one of the speakers spoke about the importance of not missing your season for certain projects. Afterwards, I was worried that maybe I had taken too long on this project and missed my season. (I actually thought that many times since then, but God was always faithful to encourage me to keep going forward.) The last meeting of the conference ended in a dinner banquet in which my husband and I sat with a wonderful family we had gotten to know at this conference. While we were at the table chatting, I learned that one of the family members had written an inspiring book himself, and I opened up that I was struggling with writing one and was hoping I hadn't missed my timing on it. This young man turned to me with a prophetic word and said he saw the story of the dry bones in Ezekiel 37 and that I should prophesy and speak over my book! I was so amazed! I quickly told him that he had certainly given me a word from God because a chapter of my book was about Ezekiel 37. I had not told them anything about this book except that it was about our nation and the Church. I knew that was God speaking to me, and I was so grateful for the much-needed encouragement. From then on, I prophesied over this book project. Therefore, I had to live this chapter. Like the scrolls handed to the Prophet Ezekiel that we read about in Ezekiel 3, which he was commanded to eat, I also had to eat and prophesy the story of the dry bones! Unlike Ezekiel, however, I didn't have to prophesy alone; God sent many faithful friends and prayer warriors to prophesy over me and this project!

We can all have situations in life that seem dry and hopeless at times, but there is nothing more hopeless than a bunch of very dry bones in need of a resurrection. Therefore, this story has always been one of my favorite "faith" game changer stories. Just think about this for a moment with me. We have heard about resurrections in the natural and the supernatural. We have heard of wonderful stories of doctors being able to restart someone's heart that has quit beating. We have heard of people being on life support and against all odds fully recover. We also have heard of many supernatural stories where a man or woman of God prays over a dead body and sees them come back to life. Jesus resurrected Lazarus after four days, and that was a big deal to Martha and Mary. They definitely thought Jesus was a bit late because they told him 'Lord, there is going to be a stench!' Jesus Himself was resurrected after three days, and His body was previously unrecognizable because of the brutality of His beating and crucifixion. However, most of the resurrection stories I have heard of do not have more than a few days that have passed. The dead bodies still have flesh on them! But, when have you heard of a real life resurrection story in which the person or group has been dead for so long that there is nothing but bones, and not just bones, but very dry bones that have probably been out in the sun's heat for many years—cracked, broken and a mess? (We do know that after Jesus's resurrection he resurrected many of the saints of Israel and took them with him to heaven. We know that Jesus will do that again at the rapture.) However, when it comes to miracles performed through the prayers of men and women of God, I have not heard of the person being dead long enough to be just bones. However, God is showing Ezekiel that nothing is impossible with Him. God is giving us an example of a worse-case scenario and showing us that nothing is too hard for our God! God wants us to believe that all things are possible no matter how long the problem has been around, no matter how hopeless the situation looks. God can always do a resurrection! Jesus told Martha in John 11:25, "*...I am the resurrection...*"

We Can All Prophesy

We must come together in unity and pray and prophesy what God desires for this nation. We can all prophesy; we don't need to be in the office of a prophet to prophesy. When we declare and pray God's will over a situation, we are prophesying.

> *You will also declare a thing, and it will be established for you; so light will shine on your ways.*
>
> Job 22:28

God calls us all to use our voices in a powerful way, which I will explain more in the next chapter. Even though my emphasis in this book is our nation, the United States of America, these biblical principles apply to any area of our lives. These principles apply to the saints living in other nations too.

Prophesy to yourself in the mirror. Prophesy over your family and friends. Prophesy to your pets. Prophesy over your home and land. Prophesy over your region. Prophesy over your nation. Speak those things that are not as though they are. Prophesy over your destiny and callings. Say, I will lend and not borrow. I will be the head and not the tail. I have greatness on the inside of me. Jesus loves me and will never leave me. I am the righteousness of God in Christ Jesus. A thousand may fall at my side and ten thousand at my right hand, but it will not come near to me. Only with my eyes will I see the reward of the wicked. No good thing will God withhold from me. I am fearfully and wonderfully made. I command every cell, every organ in my body to be renewed and restored to its best state. I will live long and see the salvation of the Lord. Prophesy, prophesy, prophesy!

Prophesy over our nation and say hear the word of the Lord: You are going to be a Godly, Christian nation AGAIN. You are going to be great again! You are going to prosper again and be a nation of great wealth. You will become a nation of revival and revivalists. You will see the glory of God covering this nation. You will become a nation of inventors and dreamers. You will be a blessing to the whole world. You will be a Joseph's storehouse. We will have righteous judges. We will have prayer in schools again. We will have a Godly and praying Congress. We will have Godly leaders again. We will have medical breakthroughs that will be a blessing to the whole world. You fill in the blank and prophesy!

Restoring Our Voices
Chapter 4

If we want to KEEP our freedom of speech, we must USE our freedom of speech!

Freedom to Speak

Have you ever been silenced? I know I have. We probably all have had people or groups of people in our lives that, no matter how hard you tried to make your voice heard, refused to listen. Maybe you were ignored, belittled, intimidated into silence, or even physically or emotionally threatened with grave consequences if you spoke up or dared to question their motives or actions. I'm not well-versed in psychology, but I do enjoy reading articles or blogs written by professional counselors when it comes to the subject of abuse. It helps me understand how situations in my own life work and helps me have wisdom on how to deal with them.

Honestly, I feel like the least qualified to talk about freedom of speech. My personality is very sensitive, and I can be shut down and intimidated very easily. I have grown and improved a lot in this area, but still have much room to grow! However, God has shown us in His Word that He never makes any of us afraid—that does not come from Him. The Bible says in 2 Timothy 1:7, *"For God has not given us a spirit of fear, but of power and of love and of a sound mind."* Therefore, if fear doesn't come from God, where does it come from? The devil, of course, and he has many people to speak through. We are all wired differently. Some people give their opinions way too much, and maybe God tells them to be quiet and listen more. Then, if you are like me, you get a lot of encouragement and prophetic words to "USE YOUR VOICE." The good news—just like minister and author, Joyce Meyer, has taught us—is that it is not sinful to *feel fear*; however, we should not use that as an excuse to back away. We can *"do it afraid!"*[1] The end result is what is most important.

I remember one time with a particular relationship in my life (a close family member) when I was on the phone listening as this person continued to bash me, falsely accuse me, and intimidate me. This was just another conversation of the same. I had become used to it. Because I knew I wasn't allowed to talk back to this person, I silently listened as I went about my business in the kitchen. When I hung up the phone, I felt like the Lord interrupted my thoughts with the question—*Why are you taking this?* I responded back with something like this—*Well, this person has trained me to do this. I know what will happen if I dare to stand up for myself.* I felt like God quietly, but firmly, said—*Don't do this anymore!*

You see, my natural personality does not like to rock the boat. I don't do well with angry people. I can be hurt easily and deeply with harsh words. Without realizing it, I had become a doormat in this relationship. I thought protecting myself meant being compliant and non-confrontational. After all, doesn't Jesus want us to be peacemakers?

> *Blessed are the peacemakers, for they shall be called sons of God.*
> *Matthew 5:9*

However, Jesus also said that He did not come to bring peace but a sword:

> *"Do not think that I came to bring peace on earth. I did not come to bring peace but a sword. For I have come to 'set a man against his father, a daughter against her mother, and a daughter-in-law against her mother-in-law'; and 'a man's enemies will be those of his own household.' He who loves father or mother more than Me is not worthy of Me. And he who loves son or daughter more than Me is not worthy of Me. And he who does not take his cross and follow after Me is not worthy of Me. He who finds his life will lose it, and he who loses his life for My sake will find it."*
> *Matthew 10:34–39*

Well, how do you reconcile these two verses? They seem opposite and yet Jesus spoke them both. Well, it is actually simple. Whenever possible, we bring peace in any situation. We practice bringing unconditional love and forgiveness to everyone. Yes, of course God wants us to love our families.

He wants us to love everyone. However, bringing love and forgiveness does not mean that we don't speak the truth. If a person rejects the truth, that is not our fault. We cannot control that or compromise our truth just to bring a false sense of unity.

In the case of my situation, I did not wake up one morning and decide I was going to be a doormat and let this person emotionally abuse me. Quite frankly, it happened over a span of a few decades. There was a conditioning. Emotional abuse is not usually a one or two-time thing. We all say things sometimes that we shouldn't. Emotional abuse is usually something that happens consistently over time. Little by little the person makes you fear them. You learn to walk on eggshells. You try to keep yourself from doing or saying the things you know that person hates. Over time, you have been silenced.

One thing I noticed is that the longer you prolong avoiding to speak the truth to somebody, the harder it is to say it. I realize now that if I had just *not* put up with certain things decades ago and created healthy boundaries as professional counselors have taught us, I probably wouldn't have been so deep in the mire. Two important things: first, whenever we ignore abuse and just keep taking it, the abuser gets used to having the control, and they get used to not having any consequences for their behavior, and the attitude in them only strengthens. In fact, the more they get away with it, the longer they have to self-justify and believe they must be right. The second thing is that the longer we procrastinate telling the truth, the bigger the fear about telling the truth grows inside of us, and the harder it is to get us to open our mouths. Truth is always good for both parties! The abuser needs to get out of their destructive behavior, and most abusers have huge denial problems. In my case, the person had even told many lies about me to friends and family. I felt the person had lied so much about me that she began to believe her own lies. After a while, she was telling the lies about me *to me*!

As most of you know, we have been in a serious battle concerning our freedom of speech in this nation and around the world. In our American constitution under the Bill of Rights, we have been given freedom of speech:

> *Amendment I: Congress shall make no law respecting an establishment of religion, or prohibiting the free exercise thereof; or abridging the freedom of speech, or of the press; or the right of the people peaceably to assemble, and to petition the government for a redress of grievances.*

Our founding fathers wanted to make sure that we were not under a dictatorship type of government that restricted our ability to worship freely or peaceably speak our opinions. Under dictatorships, many times people are jailed or even killed just for having a different opinion or religious view from their government leaders. This falls under a spirit of control that uses fear and intimidation to keep everyone under their thumb.

We have learned over the last several years that our freedom of speech which we have enjoyed for decades is quickly eroding. The rise of political correctness, woke culture, and social media censoring have infringed on our freedom of speech in our nation, especially targeting Christians and conservatives. We have had certain social media giants censor people's platforms based on a political, ideological agenda. We have seen many people censored or banned unfairly.

There is a difference between voluntary silence and forced silence. One leads to the other. Being silent versus being silenced—there is a difference. We are still in a country that *legally* has freedom of speech, but we don't want to be in a forced silence. We are already seeing the signs of forced silence with how the social media giants are treating the conservative and Christian voices. We call it *the cancel culture*; that means that your business or platform can be canceled if you speak contrary to what is deemed *politically correct* by liberal ideology. It is most definitely time for us to wake up!

If we want to KEEP our freedom of speech, we must USE our freedom of speech!

Freedom of speech is not just a political term; it is something that we need to understand in every area of our lives. Not only can freedom to express our opinions be squashed in a government that becomes very controlling, but our freedom of speech can be attacked in every area of our lives even when no one is around. You see, the devil hates the power that we have as Christians to use our mouths in a powerful way. He is *always* looking for ways to intimidate and bring fear to keep us from speaking and declaring truth. Freedom of speech begins in our thought life. *We* need to believe that our voice and opinions are important. Here are some ways the devil attacks our freedom of speech:

—— *Intimidation:* This is a form of fear that the devil uses to make you feel inadequate to speak your opinions. Intimidation can be in the form of belittling, mocking and/or making you feel too stupid to have a valid opinion. A good example of this is when Hillary Clinton called the Trump followers *"a basket of deplorables."*[2] This was her way of insulting and intimidating those of us who believe Trump was a better choice than her. (Which he *was* and *still is*!) However, the enemy can use anyone in your life to intimidate and tear you down in some way to take your voice from you. We need to resist that feeling when you think that your opinion is not good enough to be spoken. A biblical example of intimidation would be Goliath in 1 Kings 17 when he mocked and challenged Israel. Thankfully David chose to trust in God to help him defeat the giant instead of focusing on the threats. My friend, Judy, had a cool revelation one day that *"**intimidation is fake power**!"* We as God's children have the real power when we speak God's Word!

—— *Rejection/Abandonment:* This can be a subtle or an all-encompassing, paralyzing fear that someone will abandon you if you tell them the truth about how you feel about something. An example of this would be if a spouse who has been verbally abused desires to confront their spouse over their behavior but is plagued with the fear that the person will reject or abandon them if they are honest. In the biblical times of the Pharisees, people feared upsetting their leaders and being kicked out of the synagogue (John 9:22). Fearing being kicked out of a group like a church or some kind of club if you are honest with your opinions is a fear we need to resist. As long as we speak the truth in a loving and respectful way, we should feel confident that our opinions are valid.

—— *Unworthiness:* The devil is a really good accuser. He can use people to accuse you and bring up your shortcomings, or he can just throw fiery darts of accusation in your mind. For example, you may have a thought that because of your mistakes in the past (or even an hour ago), you have no right to have your prayers answered or to minister for God. The antidote to this is understanding that Jesus paid for our righteousness completely and has given us our voice back. We are forgiven of all sins when we accept Him as Savior (Colossians 1:14).

—— *Unbelief/Doubt:* The idea that your voice won't make a difference anyway is something the enemy tries to plant in our minds. This stems from not knowing our sonship/daughtership in God. We should believe that if God says we can speak to mountains and they will move, then it is absolutely true (Matthew 17:20)! If God says that we can ask, seek and knock and we will receive good things from Him, we need to trust that He is our wonderful Father (Matthew 7:7–11)!

—— *Fear of loss:* We have seen in recent years people losing their jobs over their political views. People have lost their businesses also over their freedom of religion/conscience being violated. One example that most of us have probably heard of is the Colorado baker, Jack Phillips, who was taken to court over declining to make a wedding cake for a homosexual couple because it violated his religious conscience. Thankfully, he still has his business, but he has had to fight lawsuits for almost a decade now.[3]

—— FREEDOM OF SPEECH HAS BEEN GIVEN TO US BY GOD

One day I was reading the following verse and God gave me something that really ministered to me:

> *Let us therefore come **boldly** to the throne of grace, that we may obtain mercy and find grace to help in time of need.* (emphasis added)
>
> Hebrews 4:16

I felt nudged by the Lord to look up the word "boldly" in Greek. The word in this verse comes from the Greek word, *parresia,* which mean*s **freedom of speech; confidence.***[4] I was seriously very excited to find out this gold nugget of truth. The highest form of our freedom of speech is the fact that because Jesus has paid the price for our sins, we can come *boldly* before the throne of grace. We can be confident that we have freedom of speech with our heavenly Father any time.

He doesn't sleep or slumber so we know the door is always open for us!

Also, it is important to note that after Jesus ascended to heaven and the Holy Spirit was poured out on the disciples, they spoke with great boldness.

> *And when they had prayed, the place where they were assembled together was shaken; and they were all filled with the Holy Spirit, and they spoke the word of God with* **boldness**. (emphasis added)
>
> Acts 4:31

The word *boldness* in the scripture above, also comes from the same Greek word, *parresia*, meaning freedom of speech and confidence. Therefore, we have been given boldness by God to pray and come to His throne anytime and also boldness to speak the truth to each other! The cross gave us vertical (to God) and horizontal (to man) boldness. Our gift of righteousness that Jesus paid for us to have at the cross gives us the *confidence* to be bold! Super cool!

> *The wicked flee when no one pursues, but the righteous are bold as a lion.*
>
> Proverbs 28:1

The enemy may tell us otherwise, but we do have boldness on the inside of us because Jesus, the lion of Judah, lives on the inside of us! Proverbs 28:1 is a good scripture to quote when you are **not** feeling bold. Know we have the boldness of God on the inside of us whether we feel it or not. I love to have the right feelings as much as anybody, but faith is not based on feelings; faith is based on the *truth*. We must believe what God says about us in the Word!

The opposite of speaking is being silent. Silence will not give us any fruit. If we don't speak the truth to someone who needs it, they could continue in their deception. If we don't pray and declare God's word over our lives, families, and nation, that could mean defeat. If someone is abusing you, then silence just gives them permission to keep doing it. In fact, silence gives the enemy ground, because you don't make a stand in any area.

The danger of silence is that it can look like agreement, and sometimes, it is. When someone knows the truth about a situation, such as a false accusation against someone, and they are silent, then they are basically helping the accuser. When we are silent in this nation even though we know what God's truth is, we are not helping the cause.

> *I have set watchmen on your walls, O Jerusalem; they shall never hold their peace day or night. You who make mention of the Lord,* **do not keep silent**, *and give Him no rest till He establishes and till He makes Jerusalem a praise in the earth.* (emphasis added)
> Isaiah 62:6–7

In the above verse, God is speaking to Israel, but let's translate that to America (or your own country) for our purposes here. Because God has made the saints to have dominion and be the watchmen over their country, then we can assume that God expects us to use our voices to speak the truth about Him and His desires of righteousness over our nation, and to pray and declare God's will with boldness. 'Give God no rest until…' reminds me of when Jesus told his disciples the parable of the persistent widow who kept speaking to the judge about her situation:

> *Then He spoke a parable to them, that men always ought to pray and not lose heart, saying: "There was in a certain city a judge who did not fear God nor regard man. Now there was a widow in that city; and she came to him, saying, 'Get justice for me from my adversary.' And he would not for a while; but afterward he said within himself, 'Though I do not fear God nor regard man, yet because this widow troubles me I will avenge her, lest by her continual coming she weary me.'"*
>
> *Then the Lord said, "Hear what the unjust judge said. And shall God not avenge His own elect who cry out day and night to Him, though He bears long with them? I tell you that He will avenge them speedily. Nevertheless, when the Son of Man comes, will He really find faith on the earth?"*
>
> Luke 18:1–8

God wants us to cry out to Him for victory from our enemies in our nation. We need to continue to speak truth and pray until we see breakthrough. The story above is one of persistence. An American proverb describing this would be 'the squeaky wheel gets the oil.' Let's make some noise and do some squeaking!

We need to resist the lie of the enemy that our voices don't matter, because it is the voices of the righteous that have the most power. It is especially important what the righteous say! We have the Holy Spirit living on the inside of us, and there is power when we speak—so much so that Jesus said if *we speak to the mountain, it will move!* (Matthew 17:20)

Time to Speak

> *"...A time to keep silence, and a time to speak..."*
>
> Ecclesiastes 3:7

This is the time to SPEAK. As I noted earlier, this decade of 2020 began with 5780 on the Hebrew calendar; it has been noted by many that the Hebrew word "pey" within that year means "mouth." This has been called by many notable Christian voices as a "decade of speaking."

If you want to know what God is doing, notice what the enemy is up to and flip it. The mask was a physical sign of what was happening in the spirit—the silencing and controlling of mankind. A time when God is going to use our voices loudly, the enemy is trying to silence us. A time when God is going to bring about unity in the Church, the enemy is doing "social distancing."

The devil is not omnipotent; he doesn't know everything. Apparently though, he notices when God is about to make a move; he tries to do the opposite to stop or delay the process. A biblical example of this would be when God was about to bring the "deliverer" Moses into the world; the devil used an evil Pharaoh to start killing the male babies. Of course, our biggest example is when Jesus was born and Herod began killing babies hoping he would kill the new king of the Jews. However, in both cases, God had planned ahead and kept Moses and Jesus safe.

The Importance of Prayers and Declarations

In Genesis, God commanded man to take dominion over all the earth. Since they were created in the image of God, and God speaks to create, we can assume that Adam and Eve had powerful, creative abilities in their speaking. Adam and Eve were to take dominion over the whole earth, and they were given great authority in their mouths to carry this out.

It is no wonder that the devil was quickly looking for a plan to take their authority away. Adam and Eve's decision to disobey God and eat from the wrong tree caused them to forfeit their authority to Satan. The devil is a deceiver, and he deceived Adam and Eve to believe that God was holding something back from them—that they would get more wisdom from eating of this forbidden tree. However, Adam and Eve *already* had God's likeness and image and the ability to command with their words. They would have had all the wisdom they needed and could have asked God about anything they didn't understand. They already had been given the ability to take dominion over the whole earth and were made to believe that they were somehow less than that. The devil does the same thing to us today. He can't take the authority that Jesus has given us away, but he can sure make us *think* we don't have it.

The following scripture gives us some insight into how we can use the power of our voices to be fruitful, multiply, and take dominion on the earth:

> *A man's stomach shall be satisfied from the fruit of his mouth; From the produce of his lips he shall be filled.* **Death and life are in the power of the tongue,** *and those who love it will eat its fruit.* (emphasis added)
>
> Proverbs 18:20–21

Because death and life are in the power of the tongue, we have a choice whether we want to use it for good or evil. In other words, our voices carry the power to bring positive change or negative change. Notice that there is also a *harvest of fruit* that comes from the words we speak. Therefore, it can be a harvest of good fruit or bad fruit. Bad fruit is when we hurt people with our words. Bad fruit is also when we use our mouths to spread lies, hate, and fear. Bad fruit is also when we speak badly of ourselves. For our nation, bad fruit is when we are not declaring God's will for our nation and instead only speaking about what the enemy is doing. Good fruit is to use our mouths to bless people and build them up, to pray to our heavenly Father, to speak the Word of God, and to tell the truth. Good fruit comes when we speak God's will over ourselves, our families, and our nations. We must speak life! There is a fight between good and evil over our thought life, and the result of that fight is the fruit of our words. It is important that we use our mouths to speak life and glorify God so we can be a blessing to all around us.

The following verse is an example of the power we have in prayer and declarations:

> *...If you have faith as a mustard seed, you will say to this mountain, 'Move from here to there,' and it will move; and nothing will be impossible for you.*
>
> Matthew 17:20

My very close friend, Evelyn Cutler, and I have had regular prayer times for the past several years. We live in different states, so we have our intercessory prayer times over the phone for our families, friends, nation, and the Body of Christ around the world. We love the above scripture and like to call ourselves *mountain moving buddies*. We have seen

God move in amazing ways in our prayer times. Like most of us, we have prayer times where we see quick answers and then prayer times where we are still waiting to see the victory manifest. However, we like to use our imaginations to encourage ourselves, so that we believe every time we pray concerning something, that the mountain is moving inch by inch and closer and closer to that cliff and that it is eventually one day going to fall off into the sea! The Spirit realm is different from the natural. You have to have the eyes of faith in the Spirit realm. We have to believe that the mountain is moving, and one day, we will see the manifestation. Therefore, I encourage you to adopt this vision for whatever you are praying and believing for. For example, if you are believing for physical healing in an area, believe that every time you pray about it or declare "by His stripes I am healed," the condition is getting closer and closer to its full healing! The devil likes to tell you that nothing happened, but just picture that it *is happening*!

> *Now when He had taken the scroll, the four living creatures and the twenty-four elders fell down before the Lamb, each having a harp, and golden bowls full of incense, which are the prayers of the saints.*
>
> Revelation 5:8

The above scripture is another way to encourage ourselves that God holds every one of our prayers in golden bowls in heaven. Sometimes there is a timing to answered prayer because God is working things behind the scenes that we don't see, but He is always faithful to answer us. One time many years ago, I had a dream that I was walking through the woods and found this cave. In the cave there were different chambers where different people were praying. I remember that I went into a place that I knew instinctively was the place where I had prayed many prayers. I noticed there was a book laying there and was surprised to realize that God had recorded every prayer in this book. This dream was an impactful reminder in my life that even though there are many dreams and desires that have not come to pass yet, God doesn't forget any of them. This scripture comes to my mind below:

> *So shall My word be that goes forth from My mouth; It shall not return to Me void, but it shall accomplish what I please, and it shall prosper in the thing for which I sent it.*
>
> Isaiah 55:11

When we are praying and declaring things that God has said in His Word or personally to us in prayer or even prophetic words spoken over us, they carry life that cannot return *void*. Several translations use the word "empty" instead of "void." The footnote attached to this word in NKJV says: empty, **without fruit**.[5] Therefore, we can expect good fruit to be a result of us speaking, praying, and declaring the things of God!

The story of Jericho in Joshua 6 is a great example of people using their voices in a powerful way. God told the Israelites to shout at the end of the seven days in which they marched around the city. When they shouted, the walls fell! Take notice that they shouted after the sound of the priests blowing the trumpets. I believe this is prophetic for us in the sense that President Trump for the past several years has been shaking us awake with the fact that there was deep state corruption within our government. Most of us knew there was *some* corruption, but I don't think many of us knew *just how deep it was*. The corrupt powers crawled out of the swamp to do whatever they could to destroy his presidency. However, for many of us, we got to see what was under the swamp that had been previously hidden from our view.

In the battle against Goliath in 1 Samuel 17, we read that David spoke to Goliath:

> *Then David said to the Philistine, "You come to me with a sword, with a spear, and with a javelin. But I come to you in the name of the Lord of hosts, the God of the armies of Israel, whom you have defied. This day the Lord will deliver you into my hand, and I will strike you and take your head from you. And this day I will give the carcasses of the camp of the Philistines to the birds of the air and the wild beasts of the earth, that all the earth may know that there is a God in Israel. Then all this assembly shall know that the Lord does not save with sword and spear; for the battle is the Lord's, and He will give you into our hands."*
>
> 1 Samuel 17:45–47

Notice that David spoke to Goliath that God would deliver him into his hands. David knew that Goliath was not attacking him personally but was disrespecting God. We must have this attitude when we are in spiritual warfare and/or natural battles! The battle over our nation hasn't been just because some on the liberal left hate Republicans and conservatives, but because they hate the Christian values that have been foundational to our American way of life. They are ultimately fighting against God, so we have every right to believe in prayer that God will fight for us and win!

President Trump is a prophetic type of King David, which I will explain more in chapter six. President Trump is an example of not allowing himself to be silenced. The fake news has been the voice to spread the propaganda of the Democratic party and has given him no fair and truthful coverage. Therefore, he used Twitter to express himself. He was leading the way in resisting the resistance of free speech. Yes, his tweets were not always as *nice* as many would have liked. However, he was tweeting mostly against a spirit of Goliath that not only wanted to silence him, but all of the Christian and conservative voices! Sometimes, war is messy! Even though some of the social media giants took down his accounts and silenced him that way, he has since come up with his own social media site called Truth Social. That is a type of winning a battle when you refuse to give up. We can outlast the devil if we stay persistent!

Kings Speak

We are kings and priests over America and over the earth. I remember one time many years ago, when my close friend, Judy, and I were on the phone having a time of prayer and fellowship. We both had intercessory callings and usually joined intercessory prayer groups in our churches. We had been taught a travailing type of warfare intercession, and that is not wrong—it still is necessary at times—however, on this day, the Lord interrupted us and spoke through Judy these words: **Kings Speak. You can fight that way if you want to, but all you need to do is** *speak*. Wow, all these years later, I still remember where I was standing in the kitchen when these powerful words were spoken. The Roman Centurion who asked Jesus to heal his servant understood this concept when he told Jesus that it wasn't necessary for Him to come all the way to his house, because He could just *speak the word* (Matthew 8:8–10). God has made us kings and priests.

> *And have made us **kings and priests** to our God; and we shall reign on the earth.* (emphasis added)
> Revelation 5:10

We know from scripture (Revelation 20) that there is a future millennial rule and reign which the saints are promised; however, we have been made kings and priests *now* unto God. God has not changed his mind about us taking dominion like He instructed Adam and Eve to do. Jesus told His disciples that He has given them all authority over the power of the enemy.

> *And He said to them, "I saw Satan fall like lightning from heaven. Behold, I give you the authority to trample on serpents and scorpions, and over all the power of the enemy, and nothing shall by any means hurt you."*
> Luke 10:18–19

> *Where the word of a king is, there is power…*
> Ecclesiastes 8:4

In a book I read several years ago by Dutch Sheets, *Authority in Prayer*,[6] he explains how there are different levels of authority, and the closer the proximity to your own sphere of influence, the more authority. For example, every one of us needs to first have authority *over ourselves*. We have more authority over ourselves than anyone else has.

> *Whoever has no rule over his own spirit is like a city broken down, without walls.*
> Proverbs 25:28

The above verse would not only have to do with saying *no* to our flesh if we are being tempted to do something wrong, but I also believe it has to do with keeping the devil off your physical and spiritual property. Don't let him get away with saying and doing things to you. You must speak and take authority against the thief.

Next, we have authority over our family, community, state, and then our nation. Over every area of our influence, we must pray and make Godly declarations. Our decrees and declarations are so powerful, our enemies tremble.

> *I shall not die, but live, and* **declare** *the works of the Lord.* (emphasis added)
>
> Psalm 118:17

As I mentioned earlier, my friend Judy and I have had regular times of intercession together on the phone for many years. One time we were praying over our nation concerning some of the areas where we felt political correctness was infringing on our freedom of speech. While we were praying, the Lord spoke to my friend that the reason many in this nation want to shut us up and make it politically incorrect to pray out loud and speak what is morally right or wrong is because they FEEL THE POWER OF OUR WORDS AND OUR PRAYERS!!!! They don't feel free with us here. Sometimes the enemy knows more about how powerful our words and prayers are than we do. The Lord also highlighted to my friend this scripture:

> *Why do the nations rage, and the people plot a vain thing? The kings of the earth set themselves, and the rulers take counsel together, against the Lord and against His*

> *Anointed, saying, "Let us break their bonds in pieces and cast away their cords from us."*
>
> Psalm 2:1–3

You may be thinking, "What cords?" The world is free to have their opinions just like we are. However, because we have *authority when we pray or speak the truth*, they feel bound! If they have allowed demonic spirits in their lives and we are praying against those spirits, the demons are being bound and held back, and the person does not feel free to easily do wrong and sinful things. We have been anointed by God to speak truth, and anytime we are getting a lot of kickback, know that we are most likely upsetting some demons. The reason the voices of Christians have been attacked the most is because of the *power* in our words when we speak truth. President Trump was speaking truth when he said there was corruption in Washington, and everything possible was thrown against him. The darkness never wants to be exposed but would rather remain hidden. The very fact the warfare was so intense against Donald Trump should give us a clue that there were powers that felt threatened.

Another biblical example of the enemy's fear of God's people using their authority is found in 1 Samuel 13:

> *Now there was no blacksmith to be found throughout all the land of Israel, for the Philistines said, "Lest the Hebrews make swords or spears."*
>
> 1 Samuel 13:19

The Philistines, then Israel's enemy, had somehow gotten rid of all the blacksmiths. The blacksmiths made the Israelites' swords and spears, so that would have greatly hindered their abilities to obtain weapons. Hmmm—what does that remind you of? First of all, *swords* are a type of the Word of God:

> *For the word of God is living and powerful, and sharper than any two-edged sword, piercing even to the division of soul and spirit, and of joints and marrow, and is a discerner of the thoughts and intents of the heart.*
>
> Hebrews 4:12

> *…and the sword of the Spirit, which is the word of God;*
>
> Ephesians 6:17

Therefore, the Philistines making it hard for Israel to obtain weapons could be likened to the political correctness, wokeness, social media censoring, and other forms of control that have made it hard for us to speak the truth, because *truth is a weapon*. Also, I see the blacksmiths as a type of the Church, where we are taught the Word of God. I immediately saw the prophetic significance that during this COVID-19 pandemic, many churches were either completely shut down or were hindered in their ministry. In one state, they were told *to not sing* in their churches because they might spread COVID germs. Singing, which is how we worship, is seriously important to us! Yet we hear that some places like bars had more freedom than churches. This attack is not just natural: it is a spiritual attack against God's people to silence us. Also, when you think of the prophetic significance of the removal of the blacksmiths who produce weapons, you may be reminded of how many on the left would love to take away people's second amendment rights to own guns. So we can see that our natural and spiritual weapons have both been under attack. It is not hard to see what God wants us to do when you see what the devil does not want us to do. God wants to use our voice, and the devil wants to take our voice away. It is definitely not hard to connect the dots here.

A perfect example of using the Word of God as a weapon is how our Lord Jesus handled his forty days of fasting in the wilderness when He was tempted by the devil. Every time the devil tried to tempt Jesus with a twisted lie, Jesus replied with, *"It is written…"* Jesus used His mouth to defeat the devil!

> *And He has made My mouth like a sharp sword; In the shadow of His hand He has hidden Me, And made Me a polished shaft; In His quiver He has hidden Me.*
>
> Isaiah 49:2

Therefore, we need to continue to press forward in prayer, making Godly declarations over ourselves and our nation, speaking the truth in love, and standing on the promises of God. We need to speak and declare God's goodness, favor, and blessings. Our words carry authority and power!

I love the story of Jeremiah! God took a young man and told him to prophesy to the nation of Israel.

> *Then the word of the Lord came to me, saying:*
>   *"Before I formed you in the womb*
>   *I knew you;*
>   *before you were born I sanctified you;*
>   *I ordained you a prophet to the nations."*
> *Then said I:*
>   *"Ah, Lord God!*
>   *Behold, I cannot speak, for I am a youth."*
> *But the Lord said to me:*
>   *"Do not say, 'I am a youth,'*

> *For you shall go to all to whom I send you,*
> *and whatever I command you,*
> *you shall speak.*
> *Do not be afraid of their faces,*
> *for I am with you to deliver you,"*
> *says the Lord.*
> *Then the Lord put forth His hand and touched my mouth, and the Lord said to me:*
> *"Behold, I have put My words in your mouth.*
> *See, I have this day set you over the*
> *nations and over the kingdoms,*
> *to root out and to pull down,*
> *to destroy and to throw down,*
> *to build and to plant."*
>
> Jeremiah 1:4–10

Jeremiah tried to give God the excuse that he was too young for the job. (We can all come up with plenty of excuses also!) However, God told him not to say that, but rather, to speak whatever He says and not be afraid of their faces. The "afraid of their faces" part has ministered to me for many years. One time a pastor spoke that scripture to me in a prayer line. As I said before, I don't normally like people to get angry and sometimes I can feel intimidated by just an irritated look! However, we need to look past angry faces and visualize Jesus smiling at us when we speak the truth!

God also told Jeremiah that God's words in his mouth would impact nations and kingdoms. Don't think we have anything less than what God gave Jeremiah. God has given us His Holy Spirit and when we yield to Him, God will do the same for us.

Equally important as speaking faith is listening to faith. The Bible says that faith comes by hearing the word of God:

> *So then faith comes by hearing, and hearing by the word of God.*
>
> Romans 10:17

Because we will speak faith when we hear faith, then we need to be careful what we listen to. When we listen to lies, whether it be fake news, or lies that the enemy whispers in our minds, then our faith and truth are compromised. We must keep ourselves in the truth of the Word, listen to news sources that are speaking truth, spend time in prayer, and keep ourselves in the fellowship of the saints. One of the practices that I have always had is to regularly ask God to give me truth. I regularly ask Him to not let me be deceived in any area. You see, we live in a world where there are a lot of lies, because the devil is a liar and the father of lies (John 8:44). We must be on purpose to keep our minds full of God and to be led by the Spirit concerning the voices we listen to.

— In Summary

PRAYER: Prayer is always the most important way we use our voices. Prayer changes things. Prayer changes nations. Jesus has given us authority to bind and loose in prayer:

> *And I will give you the keys of the kingdom of heaven, and whatever you bind on earth will be bound in heaven, and whatever you loose on earth will be loosed in heaven.*
>
> Matthew 16:19

SPEAKING: We must be willing to make our voices heard. No more silence. We can sign petitions and call our congressmen. We use our voices at the ballot boxes. We must use our freedom of speech:

> *…but, speaking the truth in love, may grow up in all things into Him who is the head—Christ…*
>
> Ephesians 4:15

DECLARATIONS/PROPHECY: We must prophesy and declare God's will over our nation. Declare that we are a Christian nation and that it is not going to be taken away from us. In fact, we will be more Christian than ever! Making Godly declarations from scripture or promises that God has made prophetically is a type of warfare.

> *This charge I commit to you, son Timothy, according to the prophecies previously made concerning you, that by them you may wage the good warfare…*
>
> 1 Timothy 1:18

Remember that the squeaky wheel gets the oil—so we need to *make some noise.* We need to sharpen our swords (fill our mouths with the Word of God) and declare God's promises. Ask God to fill you with the oil of the Holy Spirit. The Holy Spirit will teach you what to say and guide you into all truth!

> *And they overcame him by the blood of the Lamb and by* **the word of their testimony***, and they did not love their lives to the death.* (emphasis added)
>
> Revelation 12:11

Because of the gravity and importance of the hour in history we are in, it is vital that we use our voices to bring freedom and liberty. We must be willing to stand up for what is right.

THE THIRD DAY ERA

Chapter 5

> *After two days He will revive us; on the **third day** He will raise us up, that we may live in His sight.* (emphasis added)
>
> Hosea 6:2

THE THIRD DAY

I am truly excited to live in the days we are in. We are and will be symbolically reliving many of our favorite Bible stories as we see God bring about great deliverance for our nation and many of the nations of this world. As you see in this book, the Lord gave me many analogies concerning Bible stories and the days we are living in. This is a day of great courage and great victory!

We are currently living in the *third day* biblically. The Bible tells us how God counts days in the scripture below:

> *But, beloved, do not forget this one thing, that with the Lord one day is as a thousand years, and a thousand years as one day.*
>
> 2 Peter 3:8

Therefore, since we know that two thousand years have passed since the time of Jesus, we can understand that since we are currently in the third millennium since Christ, we are metaphorically living in the *third day* on God's calendar. We are promised in the Bible that we will be "*raised up*" on this day:

> *After two days He will revive us; On the third day He will raise us up, that we might live in His sight.*
>
> Hosea 6:2

The number "three" is very significant in the Bible. Three is a number that represents "resurrection" since Jesus was raised from the dead on the third day. The number three also represents the Trinity, the fullness of the Godhead. In addition, since Hosea 6:2 says we will be "raised up" on the third day, then the third day is believed by many to be the prophetic timing of the catching away (rapture) of the Church (1 Thessalonians 4:17). However, before that happens, I believe we will be *raised up positionally*.

Therefore, the phrase "*raise us up*" in Hosea 6:2 can have a dual meaning. It can eventually mean the catching away of the Church, but I believe that before that happens, the Church will be *raised up* in a powerful way to have great governmental influence over our nation and world. The story of Esther gives us a beautiful example of how God's people were raised up in a governmental way to save a nation.

Esther and the Third Day Church

The story of Esther is a beautiful picture in the Bible of God using the least likely to preserve His people during trying times. There is so much to glean from in the book of Esther; however, in this section I will focus on making prophetic parallels that can easily be applied to our current day and times. (I recommend rereading the whole story of Esther before proceeding since I will be referring to many scriptures in that book and making present day parallels.)

The story of Esther took place in the fifth century B.C. The fifth century is significant since the number *five* is generally understood to represent *grace* in the Bible. A couple of examples of this would be:

— The *fifth* time Noah's name was mentioned in the Bible (Genesis 6:8), it says that Noah found *grace* in the eyes of the Lord.
— In the story of Joseph, after he became second in command under Pharaoh, he showed extra favor and grace to his brother Benjamin during his reunion with his brothers (Genesis 43–45). Benjamin received *five* times more food and *five* times more clothing than the rest of the brothers. Since Benjamin was the youngest of the twelve, I believe this can also represent a last-days

generation of grace and favor being poured out upon us, God's Church.

In the story of Esther, Israel had been exiled and was under Persian rule because of their disobedience to God. However, God in His mercy and grace is always looking for a way in which He can rescue His people, even if they had gotten themselves in the trouble they are in. God will do the same for His people today.

> *For You, Lord, are good, and ready to forgive, and abundant in mercy to all those who call upon You.*
>
> Psalm 86:5

The story of Esther begins with the King of Persia, King Ahasuerus, throwing a great feast during the *third* year of his reign. Here we have another prophetic significance of the "third day" as I explained above. **One day as I was studying Esther, it occurred to me that America is currently in our *third century* since our nation's birthday in 1776.** I was excited as I felt God highlighting to me the correlation that we are in a *third day moment* ourselves and would need a divine rescue! Therefore, as we study the book of Esther in this chapter, use your imagination to see America in this story.

During the time of King Ahasuerus's great feast, Queen Vashti was holding a separate feast in her palace. After seven days of the banquet, the King wanted to show off his queen and sent seven eunuchs to go and bring her to His banquet, but she refused to come.

> *On the seventh day, when the heart of the king was merry with wine, he commanded Mehuman, Biztha, Harbona, Bigtha,*

> *Abagtha, Zethar, and Carcas, seven eunuchs who served in the presence of King Ahasuerus, to bring Queen Vashti before the king, wearing her royal crown, in order to show her beauty to the people and the officials, for she was beautiful to behold. But Queen Vashti refused to come at the king's command brought by his eunuchs; therefore the king was furious, and his anger burned within him.*
>
> Esther 1:10–12

Another prophetic significance here is the number "seven." If we count days again in thousand-year periods since Adam and Eve, we are currently in the seventh millennium since man was created. Seven is a number of perfection in the Bible, but it also symbolizes a day of rest since God rested on the seventh day. Therefore, it is significant that on the seventh day of the feast, King Ahaseurus wanted to show off his bride, but she wouldn't come.

I believe this is significant in the day we live. Jesus, our Bridegroom, is ready to show off His Bride (the Church) in all of her splendor and glory. Because we are made in His image, we are beautiful to behold. Will we show up for our King is the question I believe He is asking us?

In this story I felt that the Lord showed me some keys concerning Queen Vashti and how her role in the story relates to our day and time. In the story of Esther, when the king requested Queen Vashti to come, she was holding a separate feast in her palace and would not come. It was apparently a custom for women in those cultures to hold a separate banquet, so that part would not be unusual.[1] However, it would have been unusual and forbidden for the wife of the king to not obey any of his requests, hence the anger of the king as shown in this story. I see this as a prophetic parallel to not having priorities right when it comes to our nation or the Kingdom of God. For example, politicians are supposed to prioritize what is best for our nation and the people of our nation. When they are busy with their own agenda (banquet) and refuse to show up when needed, that can be a problem. In this day and time in America, we are truly in a battle between good and evil, and those standing for God need to be present and show up for the battle. This could represent both those in the Church and those in government positions. However, many have not shown up when needed; they were busy with their own agendas.

One of the meanings of the name "Vashti" is "that drinks."[2] I saw this as representing those in "establishment positions" whether in politics or the Church, or any other area of influence, that have gotten comfortable "drinking" the benefits of their position, instead of serving God and the people He has entrusted to them. It has become obvious that many of the leaders of the Democratic Party have unfortunately chosen a pathway that does not include standing for biblical principles, yet many Republican leaders that we expected to stand on the side of God and the Church have disappointed us also. We have had many examples of career politicians on both sides of the aisle that have shown us that they are in it for the benefits of the position (drinking the benefits), rather than to serve the American people and the constitutional and Christian values our country was founded on.

I will also point out that there can be a "Church establishment" that is not properly serving King Jesus or His people. I believe this can represent different levels of compromise. The most obvious would be Church leaders that have gotten too comfortable with the benefits of their position and have forgotten that their first priority was to Jesus and to serve the people. This attitude can cause some leaders to not address controversial issues in order to "save their position" and not lose members. However, we are always responsible to speak truth as God leads us. Since Jesus told us that His Church would be salt and light to the world, we must address the current culture we live in. The devil is way too happy to fill that void with his ideology if we don't stand up for biblical values. An extreme level of becoming "establishment" in the Church would be the Pharisee spirit that will do whatever they can to keep their position even if it knowingly hurts people and puts people in bondage.

This Vashti mentality of forgetting our true priorities in life can happen to any of us. We can all be tempted to over concern ourselves with our own problems, family, career, etc. and not *feel* like concerning ourselves with the battles God is calling us to fight. No need to feel condemnation; *repentance*, which simply means "a change of mind,"[3] is all that is needed. We just need to ask God to help us refocus on what He is asking us to do and choose to move forward.

Therefore, the king sends out servants looking for another queen, because Vashti (the establishment) refused to come. Esther, who was a young, orphaned Jew, was taken to the palace along with many other young girls. The name Esther means "*secret, hidden.*"[4] I believe that we, the Church, God's people, have been quietly hidden for such a time as this. In the story of Esther, Mordecai charged her not to reveal her identity, and therefore, the king did not know she was a Jew. I believe many of us have quietly been going about our lives, but God is choosing us to come to the forefront and be that light to our nation. Esther was taken involuntarily. It wasn't her choice and she most likely had other plans for her life. Many of us did not want this battle we have been undergoing in America. The Christian persecution that has been happening the last several years has been disturbing and has brought many of us to our knees in prayer. Those of us who would not have normally been interested in what was happening politically were awakened out of our sleep as we saw serious issues at hand.

Esther was raised by her uncle Mordecai after her parents died. The name "Mordecai" means "contrition, bitter, bruising."[5] This reminds me of the famous book, *Hinds Feet on High Places*, by Hannah Hurnard, where the guides provided to the protagonist were Sorrow and Suffering. I don't believe that God brings sorrow and suffering (the devil is good at that), but God will use the hard things that life throws our way to bring beauty, strength, and character. Such is the case with Esther. Obviously, losing both of her parents at an early age must have been traumatic, but as the saying goes, "You can get bitter or better," and she was obviously someone who chose to be better. Esther's deep character is shown in the story when we see how submissive she is to her uncle Mordecai and how she honors and respects the opinion of Hegai, who was in charge of the women's quarters. Obviously, all the women chosen to compete for the queen were beautiful, but Esther's beauty was on the inside also.

> *Do not let your adornment be merely outward—arranging the hair, wearing gold, or putting on fine apparel— rather let it be the* **hidden** *person of the heart, with the incorruptible beauty of a gentle and quiet spirit, which is very precious in the sight of God.* (emphasis added)
>
> 1 Peter 3:3–4

It is noteworthy that Esther received grace and favor more than all the others. As God's Church in America and around the world, let's also believe for grace and favor! This is something that has been particularly amazing during Trump's presidency: he has had an advisory board made up of many pastors and Christian leaders. God's people have held great influence with the Trump administration and still do as he continues to fight for America.

As I said earlier, Esther's name means "hidden." Many of us who will be used greatly in these days have been hidden and unknown. We did not come from a famous family or have huge positions or titles in the Church world. Maybe we have just been quietly going about our lives: busy raising kids, praying, and seeking God for our personal lives and families. Know, however, that God loves to raise up the hidden. Joseph was hidden in Egypt, first as a slave and then in prison, but he ended up in the palace. Moses was literally hidden by being put in a floating basket in the river (Exodus 2:1–4). Then Moses was hidden in the desert for forty years after fleeing Egypt. I believe this will be the case for many that God uses in this hour. We may not be well known to the world, but we are well known in heaven.

My Personal Hidden Story

I would like to tell you a personal testimony of what happened to me in 2020. I had been in a season of separation and aloneness in which I couldn't seem to find where I belonged in the Body of Christ like I had in past seasons. Then, in the beginning of 2020, the Lord spoke to me in my prayer time that he was about to take me *out of hiding*. I was so excited! I mused whether my family would be joined again to a church body or whether he was about to release us into our own ministry. However, what God did was amazing, but nothing like I imagined.

As you all know, 2020 started out with a pandemic that brought about many societal quarantines so many groups went online. I had already been joining in for a couple of years to prophetic prayer calls that Pastor Hank and Brenda Kunneman hosted on a regular basis for our nation. Then, one day in April 2020, there came a very unusual prophetic message from Pastor Hank while on one of their prayer calls. He prophesied that there were some on the call that were barefoot (literally), and that God was going to bring you into some new pathways in the next thirty, sixty, and one hundred days. Well, I was excited, because I happened to be barefoot! I had just painted my toenails and they were drying. Normally I would have had my sneakers on. About a week or so later, I received an unusual email that invited me to a Zoom prayer meeting for a writing class. I was so hungry for connection that without any questions, I joined what I think was my first ever Zoom call. It turned out that I was "accidentally" invited because of having purchased a writing book on Amazon from the leader of the group, Dr. Jennifer Miskov. The Zoom call was supposed to be for people who had already taken her online writing course, titled "Writing in the Glory." Well, I knew this was an answer to prayer and no accident, so I signed up for the online class immediately. Besides, I had been working on this book for years, and a writing class was an answer to prayer.

As I joined in prayer with this group from around the world, I instantly made many friends that I'm still in close fellowship with. This was the first thirty days from what I lovingly call "*the barefoot prophecy*;" I took the class, "Writing in the Glory," which was amazing, and joined their weekly Zoom group. Within sixty days, Dr. Miskov decided to do a revival course on the Azusa Street Revival. I love revival history, so I immediately enrolled in that class. I started meeting even more people that were hungry for revival like myself from around the world. By one hundred days, Dr. Miskov had officially launched a series of revival history courses which began the "School of Revival"[6] which I gladly continued, graduating from their first year school in May 2021. We studied revival history together and prayed for God to *do it again*. Boy, I'm glad I was barefoot that day in April!

Who would have thought the timing of painting my toenails would be so prophetic?

As far as the pandemic went, most of my family's schedules were turned upside down, as I'm sure was the case for most of you reading this. Both of our daughters, Ashley and Rebecca, had to graduate from college online instead of having an in-person ceremony. Our son, Kaleb, who was still in high school, was doing school online for some time. My husband, Jim, ended up working at home for a while. However, God made lemonade out of the lemon for me, and now I'm connected with some of the most amazing people around the world that are hungry for God! Dr. Miskov prior to the pandemic had these classes in person, and she lives in southern California, and I live in Georgia. Therefore, without the pandemic, there would most likely not have been Zoom classes, and there was my lemonade. The devil never gets the final say. God promises to turn everything to our good (Romans 8:28)!

I know some of you reading this had far worse situations with the pandemic, like losing jobs or worse, losing loved ones. But know that God, when we ask him to, will turn our pain into something good. So trust and declare Romans 8:28 for every loss you have had. The people that are in heaven because of the pandemic would want there to be victory from their loss and for us to continue their legacy.

Back to the Story of Esther

I believe this is the Church's finest hour, and God will be calling many out of their hiddenness. Many will feel called to political positions because of the need for us to be the salt and light and to come to the Kingdom for a time such as this.

Don't feel like you need a degree in political science or experience in politics. If God calls you, he equips you. Besides, the reason why so many of us love Donald Trump is that he has represented the common people well. He did not have any political experience. He is a businessman with common sense and that is refreshing. Those of us who have graduated with degrees in life—raising families and knowing what it is to have a budget—have learned through the school of hard knocks about the things that really matter. We have learned that spending more money than we make doesn't turn out very well. Many of the political elites have lost touch with real life and think they can keep spending money we don't have without consequences. Therefore, I think many who are hidden will arise because they have learned valuable life skills, went to the school of the Holy Ghost, and know how the real world works for the average family.

Esther rose to the occasion. She didn't pick this job. The job picked her! For us in America who have seen great erosion of our Christian values, we didn't pick this battle; the battle picked us. As soon as the liberal left started infringing on our religious liberties by kicking us off social media platforms merely for our religious and political views, shaming us for not being "woke" enough, taking Christian business owners to court just because they refused an action that violated their religious conscience, they picked the fight with us. If we care about keeping our religious freedom and freedom of speech now and for the future of our children, we must fight.

Esther could have compromised and not said anything to keep her place as Queen. After all, she had not told anyone she was a Jew. There is a saying, *"Whatever you compromise to keep, you will eventually lose."* God shows us when it is time to do something. He is waiting for us to do something. Our daughter Ashley many years ago said something profound when we were in a prayer meeting at home. She was probably in her early teens and as we were praying, she suddenly said this phrase, *"We are waiting for God, but God is waiting for us."* I never forgot that! Sometimes we have to take the first leap of faith! One of our founding fathers, Benjamin Franklin, once said: *"Those who would give up essential liberty, to purchase a little temporary safety, deserve neither liberty nor safety."*[7]

I personally have learned this lesson the hard way. As I told you before, one of my weaknesses can be "people pleasing." I have come a long way, but I still need some improvement. One day I was reflecting on some relationships in my life that I had avoided confrontation with concerning their behavior towards me, simply because I wanted to keep the peace, and would rather be the one wronged than to have to deal with their anger. I realized that it had just made their disrespect and disdain towards me even worse. In one particular relationship, I could jump through a thousand hoops and at the end of the day, they would still find something to criticize me about.

In Esther's situation, if she had remained silent, she may have continued to enjoy favor with the king for a while, but most likely, when Haman carried out his plans to annihilate the Jews, someone who knew her or her family would have called out for help from Esther and exposed that she was a Jew, so therefore, it is better to speak the truth at first. Esther went politely to the king. She was graceful and polite, but bold. In Ephesians 4:15, we are told to speak the truth in love.

I recently saw an interview with Kash Patel,[8] who had served as the Department of Defense Chief of Staff in the Trump administration. He talked about being subpoenaed for the January 6th committee, and about how in doing that, they skipped the step completely of asking him to come voluntarily. He said that he would have gladly come if asked—giving the report fell perfectly within his job description. However, with the subpoena in place, he had to pay hundreds of thousands of dollars in legal fees. He requested repeatedly over a course of six months that they release his testimony in full along with the others, but they did not. He did not want his testimony to be piecemealed together to fit their narrative. He couldn't release the transcript himself, because he wasn't allowed to talk about it at all. *He made a comment that he is not careful any longer about what he says, because he simply does not care anymore.* He would rather tell the hard truth to the American public since they were not willing to do so. I knew what he was saying and that it was a key for all of us to get the guts to say what we need to say when we need to say it. With so many false narratives being propagated out there by dishonest people, it is important that all of us are willing to speak the truth!

You see, some on the liberal left have made many of us afraid of the consequences of making them angry if we bring up certain subjects. They don't like it when we question things that they have told us to shut up about, like the origins of COVID, the vaccine mandates, and election fraud. You may even get a warning from the social media police that your account is in jeopardy.

This reminds me of how Jesus handled the Pharisees in His day. He didn't try to walk on eggshells and win them over. He told them the truth: they were like white washed tombs, hypocrites, and sons of the devil. Jesus always walked in love with everyone else. Why would He talk this way to the Pharisees? The truth is that Jesus loved them also. However, He knew they had already made up their minds about Him and their hate was so deep that only hard truth was going to penetrate. Plus, the people who followed the Pharisees needed to know the truth that they were being deceived by them.

── Significance of Haman (a.k.a. Deep State)

> *After these things King Ahasuerus promoted Haman, the son of Hammedatha the Agagite, and advanced him and set his seat above all the princes who were with him. And all the king's servants who were within the king's gate bowed and paid homage to Haman, for so the king had commanded concerning him. But Mordecai would not bow or pay homage. Then the king's servants who were within the king's gate said to Mordecai, "Why do you transgress the king's command?" Now it happened, when they spoke to him daily and he would not listen to them, that they told it to Haman, to see whether Mordecai's words would stand; for Mordecai had told them that he was a Jew. When Haman saw that Mordecai did not bow or pay him homage, Haman was filled with wrath. But he disdained to lay hands on Mordecai alone, for they had told him of the people of Mordecai. Instead, Haman sought to destroy all the Jews who were throughout the whole kingdom of Ahasuerus—the people of Mordecai.*
>
> Esther 3:1–6

In Esther 3:1, we read that Haman, the son of Hammedatha the Agagite, is promoted to a very top position in the kingdom. We can learn very much about Haman in this first sentence of chapter three. I will break down the meaning of the names:

- **Haman** means *"noise, tumult."*[9]
- **Hammedatha**, the father of Haman, means *"he that troubles the law."*[10]
- **Agag,** the king of the Amalekites that Saul spared in his disobedience (1 Samuel 15), means *"roof, upper floor."*[11]

The three names above would adequately describe the deep state in the book of Esther and the deep state in the United States of America. In the book of Esther, Haman was self-absorbed and only pretended to care about the king and the kingdom. He would later use his own money to deceive King Ahasuerus into signing a decree to kill all the Jews. It would make sense that he may have been a descendant of King Agag because that would have been a good reason for his hatred of the Jews. Even the fact that Haman's dad's name means "troubling the law" would show deep seated lawlessness in this family.

In America, we have also seen deep state Hamans emerge these last several years. I find it very interesting that Haman's name means *"noise, tumult."* The liberal left can be very noisy.

Some examples would be the rioting, crying, anger, and false accusations from liberal groups and liberal media. Many of us still have the picture in our head of the young woman screaming and crying in the street after Donald Trump was sworn in as President as if it was the end of the world.[12]

Haman can also be like the mob mentality. Haman uses fear, intimidation, false accusations, etc. to get his way. They say the squeaky wheel gets the oil, and unfortunately, sometimes it is the Hamans who are the loudest. Haman also represents our enemy, the devil. He wants to kill, steal, and destroy. He wants to silence the Church. Have you ever noticed that it is not hard to hear the devil's voice? The loud thoughts in your mind of condemnation, accusation, failure, fear, and other negativities are not hard to hear. It takes much more discipline to quiet yourself and hear the still, small voice of God whispering His goodness and love into your heart.

The fact that the name of Haman's father, Hammadetha, means "*he that troubles the la*w" is also very telling to our day and time. I don't believe we have ever seen such a spirit of "lawlessness" as today. The liberal left wants to remove borders and let criminals in. They want to legalize murder with extreme abortion laws. They want to violate our constitutional rights of freedom of speech, religious freedom, and the right to bear arms—to name just a few. This is lawlessness—no regards to the laws of our land, and especially no regards for God's laws in His Word. We regularly see examples of them calling good evil and evil good.

> *Woe to those who call evil good, and good evil; who put darkness for light, and light for darkness; who put bitter for sweet, and sweet for bitter!*
>
> Isaiah 5:20

There were violent and destructive protests that happened in many cities across America in the summer of 2020, and some on the liberal left called them *peaceful protests*.[13] Yet, on the other hand, many true patriots that truly want to bring positive change to our nation like the Trump family, Michael Flynn, and others have been painted as "evil" by many in the media and liberal left. This unfair media coverage that portrays people in light of what best helps their ideological narrative is unacceptable.

Then you have the name Agag, which means, "*roof, upper floor.*" This sounds like the "elite mentality." There are some in high positions who have become corrupt. They have decided that they know better than the rest of us. These are career politicians who have gone rogue from our constitutional and Christian values. I believe that just like Jezebel was pushed off of her high place (2 Kings 9:33), many present day Agagites are going to be removed from their high places also.

We don't know for sure, but in the story of Esther, it is likely that the Agagites were descendants of King Agag of the Amalekites. The term, Agagites, was only mentioned in the book of Esther. In 1 Samuel 15, it is recounted how many years prior, King Saul, the first king of Israel, had been instructed by God to kill all the Amalekites and their animals, but instead he had kept King Agag alive and kept back some of the best of the animals. Prophet Samuel was angry with Saul for not fully obeying God and executed King Agag himself. We are not told in the Bible whether anyone else among the royal family escaped, but since many years later we have a descendant that was called an "Agagite" with a big chip on his shoulder for the Jews, we can guess that at least one escaped from the royal family. While King Saul and his army were busy picking out the best of what they wanted to spare from the Amalekites, some of their enemies could have been given time to escape. As Tommy Tenney wrote in his book, *Finding Favor With The King*, "*Deal with your enemy now or your children will have to face your enemy tomorrow.*"[14] In other words, when we don't deal with enemies that God wants us to deal with in our present times, the next generation will have to deal with them. Therefore, in the story of Esther, we see that another generation of Jews had to deal with Haman, the Agagite, and his family.

This spirit of Agag (the elites) also reminds me of the Pharisees in Jesus's time. They were the religious leaders of the Jews, yet Jesus admonished them in Matthew 23 for not going into the kingdom and keeping their followers from entering as well. The Pharisees made themselves a spiritual ceiling and refused to let anyone go beyond that ceiling. When Jesus showed up, their jealousy stubbornly guarded their positions of influence.

> *But woe to you, scribes and Pharisees, hypocrites! For you shut up the kingdom of heaven against men; for you neither go in yourselves, nor do you allow those who are entering to go in.*
>
> Matthew 23:13

The political Pharisees and Agagites of today have not wanted America to be great or to prosper. Their stubbornness and corruption have put up a ceiling that is hard to pass through. This could include many programs of government overreach that make it hard for the average person to succeed. However, because of the prayers of the saints, God is going to remove that ceiling for us.

Notice how close Haman was to the king! He was second in command. Honestly, I did not know until the last several years how deep the deep state has been in our nation. In the last part of Micah 7:6, the Bible says, "*…A man's enemies are the men of his own household.*" In this chapter of the Bible, the prophet Micah is bemoaning the moral decline of Israel, the corruption in leadership, and the hostility and mistrust of the people among each other. We have seen similar things in America and discovered that some of the highest government positions have not been trustworthy; therefore, some of our biggest enemies were people within who have plotted to take America down from the inside.

Another interesting thing about Haman is that Haman paid ten thousand talents of silver to the king in exchange for permission to kill the Jews (Esther 3:9). Does that sound familiar? I'm thinking of some of the wealthy businessmen who have poured their wealth into radical left-wing groups that have funded some of the deep state corruption. They will use their wealth for deceitful and wrong purposes.

As the story goes, Mordecai finds out about Haman's plot to kill the Jews and sends a message to Esther that she must go before the king to expose this plot and save her people. Esther responds that she has not been called to go into the king for thirty days, and that if anyone goes before him without an invitation, they could be killed, unless the king holds out his golden scepter. In other words, Esther said she would be taking a huge risk! However, Mordecai quickly let her know that she didn't have a choice. God was calling her to do this:

> *For if you remain completely silent at this time, relief and deliverance will arise for the Jews from another place, but you and your father's house will perish.* **Yet who knows whether you have come to the kingdom for such a time as this?** (emphasis added)
>
> Esther 4:14

Esther HAD to go before the king in order to save her people. We have HAD to fight to keep this republic with our religious and personal liberties. The king would represent our government and Esther the Church. If Esther had not been willing to stand up for her people, then the Jews of that time could have been slaughtered. In present times, we have seen more animosity against Christianity than in all our time as a nation. People are offended over our prayers, over our religious views, over our right to speak about Jesus, and over other biblical truths we hold dear. We must also be willing to speak the truth when called upon.

When Mordecai confronted Esther about going to the king, he reminded her that if she was silent, God would raise up relief from somewhere else. But of course, that could have meant another generation. Do we really want our kids and grandkids to have to do this? Sometimes we can be tempted to procrastinate, to think that something will not affect us or nothing will happen yet. It would be likened to someone ignoring repeated warnings that their marriage was in trouble until one day they get handed divorce papers. It would be easier to fight for the marriage in the early stages of problems. The worse a situation becomes, the more drastic measures it takes to deal with it.

Esther agrees to go forward and asks the Jews to pray and fast for her for three days, saying that she and her maids would do likewise. God's people in America and around the world have also been in much prayer and agreement over our current battles, and we know that God is answering our prayers!

Esther going before the king was frightening. She knew that her life was at risk, but she chose to trust God and obey. Her submissive attitude towards Mordecai shows her great character. It took a lot of courage for Esther to do this. Esther had to go alone, but the good news is that we don't have to go alone. We can stand together as God's Church across this nation and let our voices be heard. And God says He will never leave nor forsake us (Hebrews 13:5).

It is recorded in Esther 5:1 (emphasis added), *"Now it happened on **the third day** that Esther put on her royal robes and stood in the inner court of the king's palace…"* I immediately thought of the Church, clothed in our robes of righteousness, taking our place and standing on God's Word. We know who we are and that we are sons and daughters of the King. We know how to come boldly to the throne of grace! Also, here is another example of the *third day*—the day of the Church! Yes, there is anointing on this! The third day is going to be the DAY OF THE CHURCH! It is the day of the Church in America and around the world. It is a day for us to arise and shine our lights brightly for all the world to see. It is the day of great victory. It is a day of celebration. It is the day of being the head and not the tail. It is the day where our enemies are terrified before us like Haman was before Esther. This is a day of favor for God's people. It reminds me of when the children of Israel asked for the gold and silver from their neighbors, and they gladly gave it to them. That was Israel's time of favor, but also the people of Egypt had fear and respect for the God of Israel.

As you know, Esther receives the golden scepter of favor, and when the king asks her what her request was, she invites the king and Haman to a banquet. After the first night of the banquet, the king asked again her request, and she asked him to come again to another banquet the next night and then she would give her request. We don't know what Esther was thinking; she may have had a clear strategy for waiting one more day to make her request; however, it is also entirely possible that she got cold feet and needed another night to get up her nerve—but hey, she did it!

I believe this is prophetic for our situation in America also. I believe it is during Donald Trump's second term that Haman will be dealt with. At the time of the writing of this book, Biden is in White House, and we have good reason to believe that the election was fraudulent. We have seen videos of the cheating, and evidence is coming out more and more each day. One of those videos is the documentary film created by Dinesh D'Souza called "2000 Mules" showing evidence of election fraud in the 2020 presidential election.[15] Therefore, when the rightful President gets put back, I believe we will see the justice we have been believing for. This is when our present day Hamans go to jail!

As Christians, we should never be believing for our enemies to be destroyed in a *physical* way. We should be praying for their repentance and salvation. However, we do want corrupt people removed from office and places of authority. We also want their crimes exposed and for there to be justice.

I think it is interesting that in Psalms 23 God prepares a table for us in the presence of our enemies. Haman was pointed out at the banqueting table. Many ungodly people want to wipe God off of our country and certainly silence all the Christians, but they do not know what it would be like for God to move back his protection. I think it is interesting that Esther told the king that the enemy could never compensate for the loss of the Jews. In other words for us: We are the salt of the earth—we are the salt of America—and if the salt loses its flavor (the ability to speak out for God) then that is not good for America. America is great because of the covenant our forefathers made with God. America is great *because God has blessed us!* If God's covenant with America had been nullified, then we would have lost our anointing for world leadership and would have become like any other nation. Like Sampson, when his hair (covenant) was removed, he became like any other man.

After Esther exposed the plot of Haman to the king, the king gave the house of Haman over to Esther to do with as she pleased (gave dominion). Also, Mordecai ended up becoming second in command. Sound familiar? Joseph ended up second in command to Pharaoh. Daniel also ended up a ruler in Babylon. I believe God wants to use these stories to encourage us that we can have Godly leaders in our government again!

Not only was Esther courageous, but Mordecai also showed much courage in this story. He refused to bow and pay homage to Haman regardless of the consequences. Mordecai refused to play the politically-correct game or compromise his religious beliefs. Mordecai and Esther both chose to do the "hard thing" because they honored God more than man. Therefore, we the Church need to refuse to play the politically-correct games and bow to the present day

"Hamans" who want to wipe us and God out of society. If we do this, we can be the Esther that preserves the U.S. (or your country) from ruin!

What if Esther and Mordecai had just wanted to fit in, to be relevant, and to not upset the apple cart? Leaders and reformers don't just fit in; they lead the way to jubilee and freedom for others.

Before the banquet, when the king could not sleep, he asked someone to read the book of chronicles to him and was told what Mordecai had done for the king. America needs to be reminded of all the good that God has done for this nation by His grace and protection. He has blessed this nation through the founding fathers, through patriots who sacrificed much for our freedom, and by prospering us and giving us the ability to move forward in great technological advancements. He has also blessed the Church in this nation by giving us religious liberties that have made us free to preach the gospel in this nation and around the world. Back in the Old Testament stories of Israel, God was always giving the Israelites instructions to remember what He had done for them. For example, He wanted them to remember how He had brought them out of Egypt and delivered them from their enemies. Therefore, we should be telling our children stories of how God has delivered America and has given us great favor and abundance.

After the king was told about what Mordecai had done and realized that he had not rewarded him for it, he saw Haman coming into the court. Haman was coming to suggest hanging Mordecai, but instead the king asked Haman if he had any ideas about how he could honor somebody he wanted to bless. The funny thing is that Haman in all his pride and arrogance assumed the king was talking about himself. After Haman got through with his elaborate idea of parading someone around with the king's horse and garments and shouting the king's honor over them, the king said, great idea!

Do this for Mordecai! *Just remember that God's vindication is always better and sweeter than you could possibly imagine!* When God gets through cleaning out the corruption of the deep state and those that had wished harm on the Church, the vindication will be worth the wait. In fact, their positions in society will be given to us!

At the second banquet with the king and Haman, Esther finally got the courage to tell the king that the enemy was Haman and that he wanted to kill her and her people. The king walked outside furious, and the Bible says *that Haman was afraid of the king **and the queen**.* Haman is a type of the devil, and we know the devil is afraid of God, the King; however, let it sink in that the devil is also afraid of God's Church, His Queen. Why do you think there is such drama right now—such hate for our President (our real one, Donald Trump), such hate for Christians? It is because Haman (the devil) is afraid of us. We are in his way. It is time that we know who we are in God. We have been given the signet ring of authority. It is time for the Church (the queen) to be respected again!

This is just an end time sidenote and only my opinion: I know that none of us know the exact time of the catching away of the Church (1 Thessalonians 4:17) except that it occurs on the third day, a thousand year period which we are only in the beginning of. However, I believe that this will be more of a celebration than a rescue event. Revelation 19:7 says, *"Let us be glad and rejoice and give Him glory, for the marriage of the Lamb has come, and His wife has made herself ready."* This scripture clearly confirms a celebration! Also, since in the beginning chapters of Revelation Jesus penned through the Apostle John letters to seven different churches in which He promised rewards to *"those who overcome,"* we can assume that Jesus is returning for a victorious, overcoming Bride walking in her God-given authority!

In the story of Esther, Haman ended up being hanged on the gallows that he had built for Mordecai. When he was about to destroy God's people, destruction came upon him instead. This is what happens to the deep state. Some will go to jail and/or lose their positions. This is a scripture that many of us have been praying for several years:

> *Let destruction come upon him unexpectedly, and let his net that he has hidden catch himself; into that very destruction let him fall.*
> Psalm 35:8

God will take up for the righteous. When evil people set traps for God's people, it is not uncommon to see them fall into their own traps.

After the king gave Esther the house of Haman, he told her and Mordecai in Esther 8:8, *"You yourselves write a decree concerning the Jews, as you please, in the king's name, and seal it with the king's signet ring; for whatever is written in the king's name and sealed with the king's signet ring no one can revoke."* Wow, they were pretty much given a blank check for what they wanted! That is what I believe God is saying to His Church right now. Believe for this kind of favor and that we will pray and decree the laws we want to have, and God will back us up! Laws in this land that are ungodly will be rewritten. Remember that the number "eight" stands for new beginnings in the Bible and that there is a double "eight" in this verse. Hallelujah! Double for our trouble!

> *You will also declare a thing, and it will be established for you; So light will shine on your ways.*
> Job 22:28

In other words, we the Church will decree what we want to see over America, not what the enemy is planning. Our words have great power and authority.

I think it is interesting that Queen Esther did not stop her requests after the initial victory over Haman and his house. She went back to petition that the damage be undone. She requested the ability of her people to fight back! I think for us, that would mean for us to not sit down just because we get our rightful president back—or sit down after we get the vindication and see people go to jail. We now have to work to see the damage the previous administrations did be undone and the laws changed. We want our liberties restored to the fullest.

We have seen examples in the Bible of "partial victories." The story of Israel conquering and entering the promised land of Canaan is one of those. They never removed all of the "ites," which became a stumbling block for them later. Do we really want only a partial victory and to only be partially satisfied? When we receive our rightful president, Donald Trump, back in the White House, that will be huge. However, if we don't all do our part to see that the laws the unrighteous wrote are overturned and work on the reformation needed in all areas of society, we could end up back in a similar situation later.

On the 13th day of the month of Adar, Haman had decreed for the Jews to be slaughtered. However, King Ahasuerus authorized the Jews to defend themselves from their enemies and to kill them. He authorized this for the 14th day also. The Bible says "they gathered together in their cities throughout all the provinces" in Esther 9:2. They came together in unity!

I found it interesting that the name Adar means "high, eminent."[16] I immediately thought of the story of Jezebel and how after she had positioned herself at a high window, the eunuchs threw her out the window to her death (2 Kings

9:30–33). Similarly, in the story of Esther, when Haman was positionally lifted up and given authority to destroy the Jews, Haman and his followers became the ones destroyed instead. Eunuchs had their ability to reproduce taken away. This reminds me of how many of us sometimes feel like we can't really make a difference because we don't have a position of authority in government or other places. However, God can use our prayers and our voices (which are powerful) to push the spirit of Jezebel out the window! Remember…our declarations and prayers move mountains!

After the Jews' victory over their enemies, they celebrated with feasts and gladness. God is about to give great joy to His Church! Proverbs 29:2 says, *"When the righteous are in authority, the people rejoice; But when a wicked man rules, the people groan."* We know what it is like to groan, but we will be rejoicing! We will have a great nation again, and that will include having great celebration and fun again!

The Mordecai and Esther Team

Mordecai and Queen Esther continued to make decrees and laws as a team. My daughter, Ashley, pointed out to me that this would represent the older and the younger generation working together! Mordecai would represent the older generation which has wisdom and experience, and Esther would represent the younger generation, with their youthfulness and strength. The two work together in unity.

When I told my friend, Luke Whitfield, a missionary in Zambia, about this chapter on Esther, he felt God speak to him about Mordecai and how important it is for men to be Mordecai's for the Esthers and bring support and protection to them. Luke was part of the School of Revival that I joined in

2020, and he was one of just a few men in the school, with most of the students being ladies. He lived by that statement by always encouraging all of us ladies in our group.

Therefore, there are two scenarios that are important here: first, Mordecai and Esther can represent two generations working together. Secondly, they can represent men and women in the Body of Christ working together. My husband, Jim, has been a Mordecai to me. He has championed me, protected me, and encouraged me in my gifts and callings. I have at times been a voice of discernment and a prayer warrior for my husband. We all need each other!

When I think of the role that Mordecai played in the story of Esther, I see their roles fitting together like hand in glove. One was not more important than the other and without both, there would not be the same outcome. First, Mordecai obviously did a great job in raising Esther with Godly values. Then, when the crisis for the Jews happened, Mordecai was firm with Esther that this was the will of God to petition the king, and she obeyed. Without Mordecai, she may not have had the courage. Without Esther there would most likely not have been an audience with the king; Esther was the only one between the two of them in a position to speak to the king. She could have refused her uncle since she was now married and moved out of the house! However, she respected his ability to hear God. Together, along with all the Jews praying, the Lord came through with a mighty victory.

I believe it is noteworthy that one of the accusations we have been facing in America lately has been the accusation that women are not being treated fairly in this country. I know that was true at one time in our history, but I do not believe that is true (for the most part) now. Women have the ability to rise just as high in the professional world as men and have equal rights under our constitution. One of the accusations has been concerning women's rights when it comes to abortion on demand. Some of those who want abortion to stay legal, being pro-choice, have been known to accuse the pro-lifers of not caring about the health of women, which is of course not true at all; we can care about the mother and the baby at the same time. The truth is that many women are traumatized for the rest of their life over regrets of having an abortion. (Remember, however, that if you are one of those traumatized, Jesus is willing and ready to forgive and heal you totally!) We have seen over the past few years pro-choice women's marches display language, behavior, and outright vulgarity that is repulsive to most Christian, conservative women and how we want to be represented as women. We are mothers, wives, daughters of the King, yet we are not *weak* as some might think. Here is a verse that I believe shows the potential strength as women we really have:

> *How long will you gad about, O you backsliding daughter? For the Lord has created a new thing in the earth—**A woman shall encompass a man.*** (emphasis added)
>
> Jeremiah 31:22

The word "encompass" in the passage above comes from the Hebrew word "*sabab*" which means *"to turn about, go around, surround."*[17] God loves using what some consider weak to confound the mighty. There will be an anointing on women in these days of not physical strength, not vulgar strength, but *spiritual strength*. We will be Esthers that use our voices to change nations. And we need and want our Mordecai's to be standing with us!

In Closing

In Esther 10:2–3 (emphasis added) we read, *"Now all the acts of his power and his might, and the account of the **greatness** of Mordecai, to which the king advanced him, are they not written in the book of the chronicles of the kings of Media and Persia? For Mordecai the Jew was second to King Ahasuerus, and was **great** among the Jews and well received by the multitude of his brethren, seeking the good of his people and speaking peace to all his countrymen."* America will be great again because God and the Church will be great again in America.

It is biblical to want "greatness" for our country! The Church of God is here to stay. This is our time for favor. We are here *"for such a time as this!"*

Let's write our own Esther story. Maybe it would go something like this:

> *In the third century of America, there was a great president called Donald John Trump. He was the 45th president of the United States of America and took office in the midst of intense political and spiritual turmoil in this nation. The citizens of this nation had been in danger of losing many of their essential liberties, including their freedom to worship. Many Christians came together and prayed fervently for God to raise up the right president for this battle and were thankful that God had answered their prayers. Many pastors and leaders were also raised up to advise our president, and they had great favor with him. However, President Trump needed more help than just the board*

of Christian advisors, because the battle was fierce. Those that wanted to stop him from making America free and great again were many. The whole church—every member—would need to get involved. President Trump was joined together with a helper called Esther (the Church in America). Esther understood the spiritual plot against her and her people and prayed daily for wisdom and help for the president.

There was a man named Haman (Deep State along with his companion, Political Correctness) who wanted to destroy President Trump and the Christian values in America. God brought vindication and uncovered the secret plots of Haman and his cohorts, and they were all put in jail! There was great peace, prosperity, and joy in the great nation of America. President Trump was the beginning of many amazing leaders that were raised up, and God blessed America greatly! Members of the Esther church obtained prominent positions in the kingdom and brought about much needed reformation! Those that felt a call to help rule the kingdom were named Mordecai's (called to the political mountain)!

We, God's Church, are in a third day era where we are to rule and reign. Get your crown on and receive the King's scepter of favor He is extending to us. This is our day of victory!

CHOOSING GREATNESS
The Bold Faith of Donald J. Trump
―――― Chapter 6 ――――

This chapter will be dedicated to our 45th President of the United States, Donald John Trump. Donald Trump is a wealthy American businessman from New York, who declared his run for president of the United States in June 2015. By March of 2016, he was the front runner of the Republican Party and ended up running and winning against Hillary Clinton of the Democratic Party. He was inaugurated as the 45th President on January 20, 2017. On his first official day in office, he was exactly 70 years, 7 months, and 7 days old. Seven is very prophetic in God's Word. It symbolizes completeness and perfection. That of course is not saying that Donald Trump, or any person on earth, is perfect; Jesus was and is the only perfect man. However, it does show that God's handwriting was clearly all over this choice for president, and that this was God's perfect timing to intervene in our nation.

It was probably the most contentious race that I have ever seen in my lifetime. It became apparent early on that this fight was a battle against principalities and powers who were contending for the soul of America. The day Donald Trump rode down the elevator of the Trump Tower in New York and declared his run for the presidency, it seemed like all the snakes came out of hiding. Deep state corruption from the opposing party went boldly after Donald Trump to destroy him. We now know that his campaign was spied on while running for president and while in the White House. One after another the Democrats came up with false accusations against him without any evidence. The fake news media carried their propaganda like they were paid staff of the Democratic party. Another reason why this was a battle that was obviously between good and evil is that real life witches also came out of obscurity and openly prayed and cast spells in public places against Trump.[1] You don't have to be super discerning to tell who has the hand of God on them when you see the devil and his followers in such distress!

At one point during the campaign, there were seventeen candidates running on the Republican ticket. I personally liked most of the candidates. Most of them expressed their concern over America, keeping our Judeo-Christian values that had been under attack. At that point, my family and I were leaning towards some of the candidates like Ben Carson, Mike Huckabee, Ted Cruz, and others who we felt represented our Christian values. I saw Donald Trump's potential to really help the nation in terms of being great at making money and helping our economy since he was a successful businessman; however, I wasn't sure about his Christian values at this point, so he was not my first choice. When Donald Trump was clearly in the lead, I began asking the Lord what He was doing? After a conversation with my friend Judy, we began to discuss what was happening. She recalled how she was exercising on her treadmill praying about God's choice for the Republicans and felt that God was singling out Donald Trump. The Lord gave her this scripture:

> *But God has chosen the foolish things of the world to put to shame the wise, and God has chosen the weak things of the world to put to shame the things which are mighty*
>
> 1 Corinthians 1:27

After our conversation, I was sitting at my kitchen table, talking to the Lord, when I began to experience the Lord's presence, giving me confirmation and scriptures that yes, indeed, God had chosen Donald Trump. I knew God had spoken and I was *all in* at this point. I trusted that God knew what He was doing.

When you look at the scripture above and the phrase, "*God has chosen the foolish things of the world,*" don't think foolish in the sense of stupidity or lack of mental prowess. Donald Trump is a genius and a highly talented individual! However, to many of the career politicians, his straightforward speech, that was not fancy and deceptive like some of theirs, was just plain foolish and unprofessional. He was often mocked by many on the left. Donald Trump did not speak "swamp" language. He spoke the truth and told us what he planned to do. I don't think any president in my lifetime has ever kept his promises he made to the American people as much as Donald Trump. And he did it while fighting numerous legal battles against the corrupt establishment.

Donald Trump, a Modern-day Cyrus

Prior to Donald Trump winning the 2016 election, Lance Wallnau, a Christian minister, was invited to a couple of the pastoral meetings that Evangelist Paula White had coordinated to allow key Christian leaders to meet and pray with candidate Donald Trump. As Lance tells the story, prior to going to the second meeting God gave him a prophetic word that Donald Trump was an Isaiah 45 Cyrus that God would use greatly.[2] At one point, he didn't remember what number the next president would be, so he had to look it up and sure enough, 45 would be the number on the jersey. Many others would also get an Isaiah 45 prophetic word. Later after he became president, even some Israeli organizations minted a collectible coin that featured a picture of Trump alongside King Cyrus to honor Trump's recognition of Jerusalem as Israel's capital.[3]

Let's look at some verses in Isaiah 45 and how they relate to Donald Trump and the season we are in:

> *"Thus says the Lord to His anointed,*
> *to Cyrus, whose right hand I have held—*
> *to subdue nations before him*
> *and loose the armor of kings,*
> *to open before him the double doors,*
> *so that the gates will not be shut:*
> *'I will go before you*
> *and make the crooked places straight;*
> *I will break in pieces the gates of bronze*
> *and cut the bars of iron.*
> *I will give you the treasures of darkness*
> *and hidden riches of secret places,*
> *that you may know that I, the Lord,*

> *who call you by your name,*
> *am the God of Israel.'"*
>
> Isaiah 45:1–3

In the first verse of Isaiah 45 above, it is clear that Cyrus had a calling not to just one nation, but to "nations." We have seen that during the first term of Donald J. Trump: he was able to not only make America much better and more successful in many areas, but he was able to secure deals with other nations that had not been done before. The North Korean Dictator, Kim Jong-Un, was someone that had been elusive to other world leaders, and Donald Trump had the first ever meeting with him in order to negotiate deals to denuclearize the North Korean country. He was able to get back prisoners from several countries, including North Korea, that others could not negotiate. I would call that: *loosing the armor of kings.*

Part of Isaiah 45:3 says, "*I will give you the treasures of darkness, and hidden riches of secret places…*" For most of my Christian life, I have wondered what that verse means. How do you get treasures out of darkness, I mused? However, I believe that the Lord has given me insight into this verse, and it came with a revelation I received one day in prayer:

I still vividly remember that day. I was upstairs in my bedroom trying to work on this book and having writer's block. In my frustration I said to the Lord something like, "*Okay I'm done trying to write this book for today, I'm going to go outside to my swing by the creek and just pray!*" Apparently, that statement of surrender and admission that I could not do this on my own pleased God because for the next two hours after I got to the swing, God downloaded to me revelation concerning President Trump and our nation as fast as I could write!

First of all, God revealed to me that He had not given us a businessman for no reason. God actually wanted to restore the wealth to America and especially to His people. It was our time of harvest as a nation and as the Church around the world. As for America, we had sown and sown to help many in trouble around the world, and we had also been a major promoter of liberty and human rights. As for the Church, the Bible says in Proverbs 13:22, "*A good man leaves an inheritance to his children's children, but the wealth of the sinner is stored up for the righteous.*" I believe we are in a season of harvest and divine wealth transfer!

I believe "treasures of darkness" in Isaiah 45:3 may refer to the wealth that the wicked have gotten corruptly, and God is somehow going to give that to us. A present day example of the corruption of wealth can be found in the history of our Federal Reserve. If you know anything about how the Federal Reserve began, you would know that it had some shady beginnings; I learned much of this myself through my husband, who read the book, *The Creature of Jekyll Island*, by G. Edward Griffin, which is a very telling and well researched book that explains how much of our wealth is currently in the wrong hands.

Secondly, the phrase "*hidden riches of secret places*" said to me that God has inventions and natural resources yet to be discovered. I know many of us probably thought that the coolest inventions and discoveries had already been made (at least I did at one time), but God revealed to me that he had saved the best for His people. Donald Trump is a leader that has a spirit of excellency. He wants to bring the jobs, resources, and wealth back to America. This is a God idea.

Another part of that download God gave was Jeremiah 33:9, "*Then it shall be to me a name of joy, a praise, and an honor before all nations of the earth, who shall hear all the good that I do to them; they shall fear and tremble for all the goodness and all the prosperity that I provide for it.*" As I read this, I felt a strong anointing that God was saying this to America. He just wants America to honor him again and have leaders that will honor him. When you read the Bible, you will see that wealth was always a blessing, not a curse. God blessed Abraham, Isaac, and Jacob because of their covenant. God does not want us to LOVE money more than Him or use it unwisely; however, again we have seen what the unrighteous do when they have the control—and as the old saying goes, he who has the gold has the control. God is ready to pour out His gold; he just needs the righteous to believe for it!

One day, our family was doing some organizing, and my daughter, Ashley, found an old TBN *Praise The Lord* recording on VHS that had an interview with the late Prophet Kim Clement along with Lance Wallnau. Thankfully, we still have a VHS player, so we popped it in and heard the interview. I was particularly impressed when I heard Kim Clement say that when God is ready to release an invention or new technology to the earth, He wants "His people" to take it and run with it. If He can't get our attention, then it could go to worldly people. I believe we are in a season where we need to seek and ask God to give us those witty inventions. We have learned what the wealthy businessmen who are not on the Lord's side do with their money sometimes and how it has negatively impacted our culture. We need those resources for the kingdom of God this time.

I found that the meaning of the name Donald means *"ruler of the world."*[4] His middle name, John, means *"the grace or mercy of the Lord"*[5] and of course, Trump means *"trumpet or drum."*[6] When you look at the meanings of Trump's full name, you can see the hand of God raising up a leader to make positive changes in our world, with the grace and mercy of God, and to sound a trumpet against corruption and wicked leaders. It has become apparent to many in the Body of Christ that we are experiencing a God-transition to bring breakthrough and Godly change and answers to prayer. The Lord spoke to author and minister Johnny Enlow that the world would be known as *"before Trump, and after Trump."*[7]

This is not to glorify a man, but merely to state that God has intervened in our nation and world, and, just like I explained in the last chapter of the Third Day Era, we are seeing the dawn of a new era because of the prayers of the saints. And just like God used a worldly king in the story of Esther along with the people of God to weed out corruption and make positive change, He is doing that again today.

Also, notice in verses Isaiah 45:2–3 that God says, *"I will go before you…"* If you count, there are three "I wills" in these two verses. God is clearly intervening; He is using specific people, as God always partners with man. Trump had a choice and obviously said "yes" to God to run for president, and thankfully, he and his family have faithfully stayed in the battle this whole time. However, God is doing what Trump or any of us cannot do—making the crooked places straight and breaking the gates of bronze and bars of iron, which I believe would represent serious strongholds in the earth. When I think of a gate, I think of something that opens or closes to give you access or deny you access to a place or person, etc. I believe there has been deep state corruption in our nation along with many other nations, that have kept our God-given blessings behind a gate, reserved for whoever controls those gates and who they choose to allow. God wants to break those barriers that have been hindrances to the blessings of God for decades. This reminds me of Isaiah 22:22, *"The key of the house of David I will lay on his shoulder; so he shall open and no one will shut; and he shall shut, and no one shall open."* We are clearly in a season where God is going to open up doors of liberty to many in bondage under corrupt leaders and systems and shut the doors to these corrupt systems.

In Isaiah 45:8 we read, *"Rain down you heavens, from above, and let the skies pour down righteousness; let the earth open, let them bring forth salvation, and let righteousness spring up together. I, the Lord, have created it."* I believe the rooting out of corruption (the Hamans of our day), will set the stage for the greatest outpouring of God's Spirit we have seen so far! Many times in history, some of the hardest and most difficult seasons precede a great outpouring of God's Spirit on His Church.

Isaiah 45:9–10 begins with, *"Woe to him who strives with his Maker…"* These two verses continue to speak of man-made idolatries. We are in an Elijah moment where the prophets of Baal are being brought down. We have already begun to see the fall of abortion with the Supreme Court's reversal of Roe v. Wade on June 24th, 2022. This was a great breakthrough against the idol of abortion, and this is only the beginning. We will see many more blows to the abortion industry along with many other idols that are against God.

Most of the rest of Isaiah 45 deals with idolatry and the revealing of the one true God. I believe that this season we are in is going to reveal God in a very public way. The number of atheists will be greatly reduced because of the glory of God that will be seen in our nation and around the world.

The MAGA King and his Deplorable Army

Recently, Biden, in an obvious effort to insult Donald Trump, nicknamed him the "MAGA King." It was a reference to the 2016 election, when Donald Trump campaigned on the slogan, *"Make America Great Again."* However, Donald Trump himself, along with many of his followers, considered it a compliment.[8] Why would "we the people" want to live in a country that is not great? We think Donald Trump did a great job, and we want him back.

What Biden intended to be a "cut-down" remark of Trump and those who follow him turned out to be a prophetic compliment. Trump is the intended God-anointed leader (king) who will "Make America Great Again," which is what God wants to do for America. He wants to raise our nation up AGAIN as a beacon of hope and light to the world, to be a promoter of good, to be a leader of human rights, to protect the babies in the womb, and to be a place where God's people, the Church, can prosper and evangelize the world. God wants to make all of us great again, and greatness and prosperity is what God promises to a nation that honors him!

> *Blessed is the nation whose God is the Lord, the people He has chosen as His own inheritance.*
>
> Psalm 33:12

BLESSED means what it says—blessed in every area! Blessed in our religious freedoms to worship our God, blessed in our heart, blessed in our bank account, blessed in our minds and not fed immoral lies and indoctrination. JUST BLESSED!

In this next section, I will explain the meaning of the "deplorable army."

The Call of King David

During the last few years, God has highlighted to me several times the significance of King David in the Bible and how there are similarities between the calling of David and Donald Trump. Let me explain:

King David was called and chosen during a time of war in Israel against the Philistines (1 Samuel 16–18). When David's father, Jesse, sent him to check on his brothers at the battlefront and to bring food to them, he heard Goliath, the giant Philistine, making a challenge for someone to fight him. The stakes were high because it was winner take all: the Philistines would serve Israel if Israel won, or the Israelites would serve the Philistines if Israel lost. We see the courage of David and his confidence in the Lord as he immediately went to King Saul and volunteered to fight the giant. David assured King Saul that God had given him supernatural strength to fight both lion and bear while keeping his father's sheep, and God would also help him defeat this giant. In the end, David took out the giant with a stone and a sling, making it possible for the rest of the army to go after the other Philistines and have a great victory that day.

Donald Trump has been called by God during a time of war. I can only speak for myself, but I had no idea how big of a war we were in until he ran for president. Like I explained in a previous chapter, I had noticed the Christian persecution getting heated up in our nation along with government corruption in many areas, but honestly, I didn't get that the sovereignty of our nation was at stake along with our basic religious freedoms and freedom of speech until a few years ago. Some people have criticized Donald Trump for being a bit rough around the edges in his speech; however, his calling during this time in history is one of a warrior. Also, as Lance Wallnau has said, *"Trump is a wrecking ball to political correctness."*[2] In a time when we are being told what we can and cannot say, we need that wrecking ball! He is called to take down the giant called Deep State, which was much larger than most of us realized. When you look at the story of David killing Goliath, you see some keys to what we are dealing with today.

The Bible records in 1 Samuel 17:4–7 that Goliath was six cubits and a span high and that his iron spearhead weighed six hundred shekels. Later, while King David was in power, some of his warriors killed four other giants, and one is recorded as having six fingers on each hand and six toes on each foot (2 Samuel 21:20). The significance of the number six is recorded in Revelation 13:18 as the number of the beast, which was also the number of man, 666. I believe this would be symbolic of the antichrist spirit. Before any future revealing of an ultimate Antichrist takes place, the Bible makes it clear that the spirit of the antichrist is already here.

> *…and every spirit that does not confess that Jesus Christ has come in the flesh is not of God. And this is the spirit of the Antichrist, which you have heard was coming,* **and is now already in the world.** (emphasis added)
>
> 1 John 4:3

Much of the liberalism we have been dealing with in society today operates in an "antichrist spirit." This spirit wants to push Godly values out of America, out of education, out of the medical field, and out of the family, along with many other areas of society. The whole push for abortion is against biblical values (Psalm 139:13–16). The push to expose young children to inappropriate sexual teaching against the will of their parents is evil. Every push to legislate immorality that is against God and how He made us is antichrist.

Therefore, if you look at this comparison, just like King David was called to take down a giant that was evil and there were a lot of "sixes" associated with these giants, we can assume that King David and his men were not just coming against *extra tall* warriors—these giants were the embodiment of evil, with antichrist spirits that were coming against God and His plan for His people, Israel. We can easily connect the dots here to find that President Trump has a similar commission as King David. The deep state is a type of a Goliath, with an antichrist spirit that wants to destroy America and the Christian values America has held dear for centuries. This Goliath antichrist spirit is not just here in America: we have seen similar battles all over the world and have good reason to believe that our deep state is connected to many other deep states in other countries. This has been no insignificant battle; I believe this will be known as one of the most important battles in history. The devil clearly wanted to take down the Christian and righteous influence America has had on the world and bring a one-world agenda that would usher in the ultimate Antichrist. However, this is not the devil's time; this is God's time! This is the promised season that many have prophesied about in which God's glory will be poured out on the earth. These are the days of the "greater works" that Jesus promised us in John 14:12. God wants as many people to follow him as possible; therefore, God wants His people to have great favor and victory in order to have great influence for the kingdom of God. Many have had prophetic words and visions that God's greatest revival and outpouring as of yet is on the horizon. This is the "Third Day Era" as I called it in the previous chapter in which I highlighted the story of Esther.

Another common thread here is that King David was very zealous for his country, Israel:

> *Then David spoke to the men who stood by him, saying, "What shall be done for the man who kills this Philistine and* **takes away the reproach from Israel***? For who is this uncircumcised Philistine, that he should defy the armies of the living God?"* (emphasis added)
>
> 1 Samuel 17:26

King David saw it as shameful how Israel was being dishonored by Goliath and the Philistines. The spirit of Goliath is one of intimidation. Goliath was intimidating by *his words*. This brought fear to the people of God. In this story, we never read Goliath actually physically attacking any of the Israelites, but he attacked through his words of insult, condemnation, shame, and accusation. We hear those voices today.

This reminds me of how Donald Trump took notice and was bothered by the fact that some of the other countries were disrespecting us and taking advantage of us financially by pushing unfair trade deals, paying less than their fair share to NATO, along with creating other imbalances. He has also been very vocal about the dishonesty of many news outlets. The lying and accusatory spirit many of the fake news outlets operate in is a type of the Goliath spirit—using words to attack.

Just like King David was zealous for Israel, Donald Trump is passionate about this nation. One of the areas of passion he has is in our military. He didn't like it when he noticed that our military was depleted of adequate equipment and transportation. Trump made great progress in this area during his first term of presidency. Making America great again was Trump's way of saying that he loved our country!

Another important note is that even though King David knew he had been anointed and chosen by God through the Prophet Samuel, it took many years for this to come to pass as he was hunted down by King Saul. King Saul once loved David after he killed the giant and also became part of his household; however, when he noticed the people's favoritism towards David—he heard the crowds sing a song that said Saul has killed his thousands and David his ten thousands—a spirit of jealousy came upon Saul (who would represent the political establishment), and Saul spent years trying to kill David.

We know that President Trump has experienced a similar level of persecution. During Trump's entire first term in office until now, the deep state (Saul) has chased him with false legal scandals, trying to destroy his presidency. The hate was at a murderous level in which they would try every trick they knew to get rid of him and destroy his family, his wealth, and his reputation. However, Donald Trump is no quitter. He is still fighting for our country. For that, we should be very thankful that he and his family have been willing to do that!

During the time King David was running from Saul, he amassed his own army that followed him. The Bible says in 1 Samuel 22:2 (emphasis added), *"And everyone who was in **distress**, everyone who was in **debt**, and everyone who was **discontented** gathered to him. So he became captain over them. And there were about four hundred men with him."* I heard Pastor Joseph Prince of New Creation Church in Singapore call this the "3 'D' Army" in one of his sermons.[9] In 1 Samuel 23, the Bible calls this army *the mighty men of David* and lists the great exploits they had done.

As I mentioned previously, Hillary Clinton had once called the followers of Trump a *"**basket of deplorables**!"*[10] One day when I was thinking about this, I realized it was significant that "deplorables" also begins with the letter "d". Let's look at the dictionary definition of deplorable:[11]

— causing or being a subject for grief or regret; lamentable:
— causing or being a subject for censure, reproach, or disapproval; wretched; very bad

I thought the definition above was very telling. In simple terms, they don't like us! However, a couple of words jumped out at me: "censure and disapproval." Isn't it true that many conservative, Christian people have been kicked off social media platforms (censured), for having an opinion or ideology that those on the left disapprove of? Some people have actually been fired from a job if they are found out to be a Trump supporter!

Therefore, some on the left see us as the *"Army of the Deplorables."* However, I would like to think we are likened to the *"Mighty Men of David."* Just like I wrote about in chapter two highlighting Gideon and his army of 300, God called Gideon, who had low self-esteem, *mighty*! I believe God sees those of us praying and standing with God over this nation "mighty warriors!" And if you want to compare us to those in distress, debt, and discontented, like the mighty men of David, I would liken that to this: many of us are *distressed* at the corruption in our country, many of us do not make up the rich in this country— we are ordinary people with a house mortgage, car payment, and possible other *debt*—and we are definitely *discontented* with how things are going in our country—open borders, high gas prices, food shortages, etc. We want to "**Make America Great Again**."

── Choosing Greatness ──────────────

Do you know that "greatness" is a choice? In Deuteronomy 28:1–14, God tells the people of Israel what their blessings will be if they follow Him and obey Him. Then, in verses 15–68, God explains what their curses will be if they don't follow Him. After God was through carefully explaining to them their choices, He actually gives them the answer to the quiz in case they still didn't understand:

> *I call heaven and earth as witnesses today against you, that I have set before you life and death, blessing and cursing; therefore* **choose life**, *that both you and your descendants may live* (emphasis added)
>
> Deuteronomy 30:19

One day in a prayer time with my close friend, Evelyn, she brought to my attention that Donald Trump speaks in declarations. He speaks faith talk! "I want to make America great again" is faith talk. When the economy was at its best, and then we took a hard hit with COVID-19, Trump promised that we will build the economy back strong *again*.[12] He has a mentality that all things are possible. He speaks those things that are not as though they are (Romans 4:17)!

I'll never forget President Trump's second State of the Union Address on February 5th, 2019. As he was making closing remarks, he said these words:

> *Together we represent the most extraordinary nation in all of history. What will we do with this moment? How will we be remembered? I ask the men and women of this Congress, look at the opportunities before us. Our most thrilling achievements are still ahead. Our most exciting journeys still await.*
>
> *Our biggest victories are still to come. We have not yet begun to dream. We must choose whether we are defined by our differences or whether we dare to transcend them. We must choose whether we squander our great inheritance or whether we proudly declare that we are Americans. We do the incredible. We defy the impossible. We conquer the unknown.*
>
> *This is the time to reignite the American imagination. This is the time to search for the tallest summit and set our sights on the brightest star. This is the time to rekindle the bonds of love and loyalty and memory that link us together as citizens, as neighbors, as*

> *patriots. This is our future, our fate, and our choice to make. I am asking you to* **CHOOSE GREATNESS.** *No matter the trials we face, no matter the challenges to come, we must go forward together. We must keep America first in our hearts. We must keep freedom alive in our souls. And we must always keep faith in America's destiny. That one nation under God must be the hope and the promise and the light and the glory among all the nations of the world.*
>
> *Thank you, God bless you. And* **God bless America.** *Thank you very much.* (emphasis added)[13]

Donald Trump has chosen greatness for our country. The question remains whether "we the people" of this great nation will choose greatness. One president cannot do that alone. It will take God's people to pray, choose, and stand for God's plan of greatness for our country. And this also goes for everyone reading this from other countries. Believe for your country also to receive God's will and great plan!

Gathering Together on the Wall
Responding to the Sound of the Trumpet
Chapter 7

> *I have set watchmen on your walls,*
>   *O Jerusalem;*
> *They shall never hold their peace day or night.*
> *You who make mention of the Lord,*
>   *do not keep silent*
>
> Isaiah 62:6

The Church is the watchmen on the walls, and we should not be silent in prayer for America, nor should we be silent in speaking truth. We should be the voice of discernment in this nation and the voice of prayer, fighting spiritual battles.

A watchman is someone who stands guard on the walls around a city, military fort, or nation, to watch for any possible enemies that may try to sneak in. If they see enemies, they will alert others to fight. A "watchman" would also describe the people who used to patrol the streets of a city at night to watch for criminal activity or for fires. These people were replaced by police in the mid-1800s. In whatever form they took, having a watchman around to keep people safe was crucial!

As spiritual watchmen, we are watching in "prayer" and using our "voices." Prayer gives us the ability to see from heaven's perspective what is happening in the earthly realm. In Ephesians 6:12 we read, *"For we do not wrestle against flesh and blood, but against principalities, against powers, against the rulers of the darkness of this age, against spiritual hosts of wickedness in the heavenly places."* We need to use our voices to pray and decree what God's will is for every situation. We also need to use our voices to tell others what God is saying to us.

I love the scripture in Matthew 16:19, *"And I will give you the keys of the kingdom of heaven, and whatever you bind on earth will be bound in heaven, and whatever you loose on earth will be loosed in heaven."* God has given His Church His keys with the authority to prohibit certain things and allow certain things. As watchmen on the walls, we should be in prayer, prohibiting the demonic from entering what we are in charge of (our nation) and praying and allowing God's presence to be welcome. It is a very important job we have!

── Nehemiah and the Building of the Wall

In our nation, Donald Trump and many others have wanted to build a wall on our southern border because of people entering illegally. There has been much heated debate over this topic. I found there were parallels to what we are currently living through in the story of Nehemiah in the Bible. Nehemiah's story took place in approximately 423 B.C. He was a cupbearer to King Artaxerxes of Persia.

> *And they said to me, "The survivors who are left from the captivity in the province are there in great distress and reproach. The wall of Jerusalem is also broken down, and its gates are burned with fire."*
>
> Nehemiah 1:3

Hanani was one of the brethren from Judah who came and gave Nehemiah the report above concerning the state of Jerusalem. The name Hanani means "my grace, my mercy." [1] God was bringing grace and mercy to Jerusalem, and He is now bringing grace and mercy to America!

Nehemiah was devastated to find out that Jerusalem was in ruins and requested that the king allow him to return for a period of time to Judah to help rebuild it, and he was granted favor to go.

While Nehemiah was still on his way and had given letters to officials in the region from the king, we get a glimpse of who will be the two villains in this story:

> *When Sanballat the Horonite and Tobiah the Ammonite official heard of it, they were deeply disturbed that a man had come to seek the well-being of the children of Israel.*
>
> Nehemiah 2:10

I thought the above verse was prophetically significant in the fact that Donald Trump has had an America-first emphasis—wanting to care about the American people first. However, some on the liberal left have acted "deeply disturbed" that he wanted to put American citizens first. Hmm, what is wrong with this picture?

The name "Sanballat" means *bramble-bush; enemy in secret*.[2] A bramble bush is a rough, tangled, prickly shrub which could represent to us the tangled web of deceit and lies that we have seen. The meaning "enemy in secret" can represent to us the deep state and media. They pretend to be for the people, but secretly they have aligned themselves to do evil. The name "Tobiah" means *goodness of Jehovah*.[3] Obviously in this story, Tobiah was not representing his name. However, we do see some on the liberal left at times move in a Pharisee and religious spirit. They can pretend to care about people, but later, you see their real motives come out. A good example of this is how they push pro-abortion rhetoric by using phrases like "women's health." That sounds good on the surface, because everyone wants a woman to be healthy, but they are leaving out the part that there is a real person (sometimes fully formed already) in the womb that will be killed. This is a deceptive way of pretending to "care about women." We have even seen them occasionally pull out a Bible scripture used in a wrong context to try to justify something wrong they are doing. But then again, that should not be a big surprise. Even the devil improperly used Bible scriptures to try to trip up Jesus when he was being tested in the wilderness (Luke 4:1–13).

Therefore, when I read about Sanballat and Tobiah in the story of Nehemiah, I immediately saw them today represent the *fake news media buddies* and of course the *deep state in general* which would refer to government officials in high ranking positions that are doing illegal and anti-constitutional dealings in secret. Tobiah would also represent the Pharisee side of this which is pretending to care about people when there is really a serious evil agenda going on.

After Nehemiah spoke his plan to his fellow Jews that they rebuild the wall, he received a bit of pushback and warfare like Donald Trump did!

> *Then I said to them, "You see the distress that we are in, how Jerusalem lies waste, and its gates are burned with fire. Come and let us build the wall of Jerusalem, that we may no longer be a reproach." And I told them of the hand of my God which had been good upon me, and also of the king's words that he had spoken to me.*
>
> *So they said, "Let us rise up and build." Then they set their hands to this good work.*
>
> *But when Sanballat the Horonite, Tobiah the Ammonite official, and Geshem the Arab heard of it, they laughed at us and despised us, and said, "What is this thing that you are doing? Will you rebel against the king?"*
>
> *So I answered them, and said to them, "The God of heaven Himself will prosper us; therefore we His servants will arise and build, but you have no heritage or right or memorial in Jerusalem."*
>
> Nehemiah 2:17–20

What I love about the story of Nehemiah is that despite the warfare and mockings from their enemies, they kept building the wall, and they did it in unity. In fact, because of the threats from their adversaries, they had to hold a construction tool in one hand and a weapon in the other (Nehemiah 4:17). The truth is that the enemy (the devil) always tries to hinder and discourage the people of God when we move forward in the dreams and assignments that the Lord gives us. For us our weapon is spiritual in prayer, and natural in using our freedom of speech and whatever else God tells us to do.

One of the verses in Nehemiah that stood out to me the most was this:

> *Then I said to the nobles, the rulers, and the rest of the people, "The work is great and extensive, and we are separated far from one another on the wall. Wherever you hear the sound of the trumpet, rally to us there. Our God will fight for us."*
>
> Nehemiah 4:19–20

I couldn't help but think of how the Body of Christ is sometimes separated from each other when we desperately need one another—especially in a war. I felt a prophetic anointing on this as these words came alive to me: *Whenever you hear the sound of the trumpet (Trump) rally to us there. Our God will fight for us.* I believe along with many others that we are at a pivotal point in history where God wants His people to learn to work together in this battle. It does not mean we have to agree on everything, but Trump was our cue to stand together for our country.

When I think of "walls," I think of a few different meanings:

—Walls are a sign of protection and safety. A wall is built to keep intruders out.
—Walls are also indicative of the word "boundaries." God's Word teaches us healthy boundaries in relationships and healthy

boundaries in our lifestyle habits. God wants us to be safe from sinful habits that would destroy our lives. He also wants us to have boundaries in choosing relationships so that we may be equally yoked together (2 Corinthians 6:14).

— In a national way, walls are a symbol of the sovereignty of our nation. The walls that President Trump and others have wanted to build on our southern border is a good thing. It tells other people and nations that if they want to come here, they need to go through the proper channels and come legally, not illegally. That is just plain common-sense. You expect a stranger to knock on your front door or ring the doorbell and wait for you to "invite them in." It is not okay to come into your house uninvited.

— One negative connotation I think of with "walls" is when you put up walls to separate or divide yourself from others in relationships. Fear of rejection, fear of abandonment and others are types of walls we must take down so we can walk in love and truth with people.

— Another negative result of "walls" is the divisions in the Body of Christ. But I will speak more about that in the next chapter.

Therefore, like many things, walls can be good or bad. It is just how you use them. If they are used for healthy boundaries and protection (like, in my opinion, the southern border), then that is the right thing to do, because a good parent wants to protect their family; that's why we lock our doors at night! If you are using personal walls to self-protect out of fear, like I described concerning myself in the

Restoring Your Voices chapter, then we need to ask God to help us remove those walls.

—— Even God Has Walls and Boundaries ——

Psalm 91:1–2 says, *"He who dwells in the secret place of the Most High shall abide under the shadow of the Almighty. I will say of the Lord, 'He is my refuge and my fortress; My God, in Him I will trust.'"* God puts spiritual walls of protection around those of us who put our trust in Him. In fact, that was a complaint that the devil had against God concerning Job: we see recorded in Job 1:10, *"Have You not made a hedge around him, around his household, and around all that he has on every side? You have blessed the work of his hands, and his possessions have increased in the land."* The devil was angry and frustrated that he could not have free access to destroy Job! In a world that is asking for "safe spaces," there is no safer space than the presence of God in our lives!

Even God has a wall around the heavenly Jerusalem described in detail in Revelation:

> *And he carried me away in the Spirit to a great and high mountain, and showed me the great city, the holy Jerusalem, descending out of heaven from God, having the glory of God. Her light was like a most precious stone, like a jasper stone, clear as crystal. Also she had a **great and high wall** with twelve gates, and twelve angels at the gates, and names written on them, which are the names of the twelve tribes of the children of*

> *Israel: three gates on the east, three gates on the north, three gates on the south, and three gates on the west.* (emphasis added)
>
> Revelation 21:10–13

The Finishing of the Wall

The good news is that war doesn't last forever. Building projects don't last forever, and it is really a good feeling to be able to say like Nehemiah:

> **So the wall was finished…** (emphasis added)
>
> Nehemiah 6:15

Many times in our lives a particular thing or place can represent both something natural and spiritual. When it comes to the fact that we have been trying to build a wall in our nation to keep out possibly dangerous people and keep our people safe, I think of what God is doing spiritually in America. We began our country with a covenant with God. Our founding fathers made laws that represented biblical values. That was the "wall" around our nation, but we have seen many of our foundational and biblical values being torn and broken down. As the Church in America, we are the watchmen on the walls over this country. We want to see God's wall of supernatural protection over our country along with a wall that represents biblical boundaries. I believe as we do this we have a promise of revival coming to our nation:

> *…Do not let the gates of Jerusalem be opened until the sun is hot…*
>
> Nehemiah 7:3

As I read this, I immediately saw that "the sun is hot" as representing "the Son, Jesus" and the Church being hot (passionate) for him—not lukewarm, but hot! I immediately heard in my heart "**until there is revival.**" Let's not stop what we are doing until we see major revival in this nation! There is a great outpouring about to come!

As we continue to move forward, let's remember what Nehemiah said to the Jews:

> *…Do not sorrow, for the joy of the Lord is your strength.*
>
> Nehemiah 8:10

Let's always be mindful that when the enemy tries to steal our joy, he gets our strength. Pay no attention to the fake news media buddies and their deep state companions. Hopefully they will learn their lesson and come join Team Jesus! If not, Team Jesus is going to replace them with truthful news outlets and honest politicians. It is their choice to make. However, we will keep our joy because we are on the winning team!

THE TALE OF TWO TOWERS
The Blessings and Power of Unity
Chapter 8

— KINGDOM OF GOD VS THE KINGDOM OF DARKNESS

Several years ago, my close friend, Judy, and I were having one of our regular intercessory prayer times on the phone. We were in prayer for our nation when Judy suddenly had a vision of "*two towers*". She immediately knew that one tower represented the kingdom of God and the other one represented the kingdom of darkness. Shockingly, in the vision, the kingdom of darkness's tower was much taller than the one representing the kingdom of God. Now, we all know that God Himself is ALWAYS way more powerful than the devil, but this vision represented the *influence* (authority and dominion) that God's Church (God's family on earth) were having over our nation and world versus the *influence* the kingdom of darkness (corrupt people in unity) were having over our nation and world. Judy sensed when she saw this vision that the enemy's camp was way more organized and unified than God's people, and God wanted this to be changed. We began praying regularly for God's people to arise and take their places of authority and rule as we were always supposed to do, walking in the power of unity that would bring defeat to the kingdom of darkness.

This vision and prayer time was before Donald Trump got elected in 2016; as I said earlier, we had no idea how organized the darkness had really been. We knew what God had shown us in the Spirit, but in the natural, we didn't know the details. Since then we have found out more and more about the deep state corruption that has been going on for a long time and was very coordinated between many groups and even nations. When Donald Trump rode down that elevator to announce he was running for president, we saw the beginnings of just how organized they were.

Since that time several years ago, I have seen God's people rise to the occasion, and I believe that our tower right now is WAY HIGHER than the one on the dark side. We have seen great prophetic voices take their place to speak God's truth to our nation. We have seen prayer groups rise up all over the world to take their places in the battle. Many Christians who were not involved in politics have felt a call to be part of bringing God's kingdom to that arena. Christian and conservative news programs have arisen to take their place of speaking truth. I believe our tower of light is becoming stronger and taller each day, and we will witness the fall of the dark tower very soon. Its days are numbered. In fact, we can hear the beginning sounds of that tower crumbling now, and great will be its fall!

We know now that corrupt people in government and other places planned a coordinated spying attack on Trump and his campaign and even tried to frame him on Russian collusion based on a false and phony document paid for by the Democratic Party.[1] The fake news media sang the same song daily all in unison: *Tell me lies, tell me sweet little lies…* (For those of you who are too young to know the song I just referenced, that was a song in the '80s sung by Fleetwood Mac titled "Little Lies"). We heard, "Russia, Russia, Russia, Russia" repeatedly. However, the truth is that they were not *little* lies and definitely not *sweet*.

Tower of Babel

> *Now the whole earth had one language and one speech. And it came to pass, as they journeyed from the east, that they found a plain in the land of Shinar, and they dwelt there. Then they said to one another, "Come, let us make bricks and bake them thoroughly." They had brick for stone, and they had asphalt for mortar. And they said, "Come, let us build ourselves a city, and a tower whose top is in the heavens; let us make a name for ourselves, lest we be scattered abroad over the face of the whole earth."*
>
> *But the Lord came down to see the city and the tower which the sons of men had built. And the Lord said, "Indeed the people are one and they all have one language, and this is what they begin to do; now nothing*

> *that they propose to do will be withheld from them. Come, let Us go down and there confuse their language, that they may not understand one another's speech." So the Lord scattered them abroad from there over the face of all the earth, and they ceased building the city. Therefore its name is called Babel, because there the Lord confused the language of all the earth; and from there the Lord scattered them abroad over the face of all the earth.*
>
> Genesis 11:1–9

The Tower of Babel is an example of the kingdom of darkness. They were in such unity, but it was unity against God, not for Him. Their unity was such a serious threat that it got God's attention enough to get out of His seat and do something about it. There appears to be only two incidents that we read of in the Old Testament in which God had to intervene in a *major way* to keep His plan going for mankind. The first one is, of course, Noah's Ark and the flood. The Bible says their thoughts were only evil continually, so God had to intervene with a flood to destroy most of mankind to preserve the human race. The second would be the Tower of Babel in which whatever was happening was so serious, God had to break their unity up and confuse their language. We do know scientifically that their tower of bricks and mortar was *not* going to reach heaven; they would run out of oxygen *way* before then! Therefore, we have to assume that the Tower of Babel was doing something *spiritually dark* that would have affected mankind in a majorly negative way.

Another significant detail of this story is that those building the Tower of Babel "*wanted to make a name for themselves and for their tower to reach heaven.*" This to me compares to the attitude of Lucifer before he got kicked out of heaven:

> *"How you are fallen from heaven,*
> *O Lucifer, son of the morning!*
> *How you are cut down to the ground,*
> *you who weakened the nations!*
> *For you have said in your heart:*
> *'I will ascend into heaven,*
> *I will exalt my throne above the stars of God;*
> *I will also sit on the*
>   *mount of the congregation*
> *on the farthest sides of the north;*
> *I will ascend above the heights of the clouds,*
> *I will be like the Most High.'*
> *Yet you shall be brought down to Sheol,*
> *to the lowest depths of the Pit."*
>
> Isaiah 14: 12–15

Let's look at the correlation here. The devil wanted to exalt his throne above God's throne; he wanted to be worshiped. This is pride and self-exaltation. The kingdom of darkness is opposite to the kingdom of God. God teaches us to be humble, saying that the greatest among you will serve (Matthew 23:11). In the kingdom of God, He wants *everyone* to excel and have their best life possible!

The devil usually copies God's principles of unity but is doomed to fail, because real unity takes *"loving one another."* In John 13:35, Jesus said, *"By this all will know that you are My disciples, if you have love for one another."* This is real unity, in which there is love for God and love for each other. The devil has "fake unity" because it is not based on love, but is on a faulty foundation of selfishness which always eventually crashes. Those in darkness will quickly turn on each other when things don't go well with their wicked plan.

We have over the last few decades seen a rise of what I will call *"The Tower of Fake News."* We have seen many media outlets along with many social media giants coming together in a *fake unity*. How do we know this? Because they are all saying the same lies over and over again. I have seen video clips from conservative news hosts showing many media outlets all saying the same lie that particular day with the same or similar wording, like they had all received the same memo in their email box! Babel means "confusion," and these lies being told have caused a lot of confusion in people's lives of not knowing what to believe.

The tower of darkness has also been promoting a FAKE AWAKENING. A fake awakening is called **"woke."** We must know the difference between the fake awakening and the real awakening. This "woke" has a yoke of bondage attached. It comes with a heavy price of taking away our liberty and our freedoms. It is the kind of "woke" that Eve bought into when she ate of the wrong tree—her eyes were opened, but to the wrong news network. (Just a little humor here.) She needed to have partaken of the tree of life that is full of truth, life, and true liberty. The devil's lies can contain some "truth," but it is a perverted truth. It is spun with deceit and deception.

We are in a new day where we have to choose carefully what we listen to. News is no longer the facts of the days. Many times it is the enemy's news, not God's news. We must choose carefully from now on. It is important that you ask God for truth. Ask Him for discernment. Ask Him to reveal any kind of deception in your life. Ask Him to show you the right people or groups to listen to. We must be followers and lovers of truth.

A Story of Bad Fruit from Fake News

I'm going to tell you a personal story of what listening to fake news can do to a person. The grocery store that is up the street from me previously had a man probably in his sixties bagging groceries that I really enjoyed talking to. He was always laughing and was very friendly with all the customers. He used to call me his "VIP customer" because I came often—I live right down the street. One day I noticed that I had not seen him in a while. I was concerned and started praying for him. I missed his happy face! Then one day many months later I happened to run into him while shopping at Sam's Club. This man happened to be walking down an aisle that I was on, and we began to talk. I was excited to see him and felt like it was an answer to prayer. I told him that I missed him and asked how he was doing. He said he had retired because he had to have hip replacement surgery; he was there shopping with his wife. He said that since he retired he just sits at home and watches a Certain News Network that I consider "fake news."

Well, next thing you know, his face contorted with anger, and he started talking about President Trump. He kept saying how much he hated him. He has liked every president but him! This was a man that *always* seemed to be friendly, joyful, and kind, and I was standing there a bit shocked at the rage in which he began to speak. I said that I was *for* President Trump, and then he put his hand out to not let me speak and continued saying again how much he hated him. I could tell there was a demonic influence over him, and I began to pray under my breath. I hoped that maybe if I could put my hand on his back and pray, that maybe that hate would melt off. I asked him if he was a Christian and he said yes, but that he could forgive anyone in the U.S., but not Trump. He started repeating fake news he had heard on this particular news network. It just goes to prove that it is much more than false information being propagated. There is actually a *spirit of hate* being released out in the airways. It reminded me of cartoons when you see a character's face turn red with smoke rising from their ears! It was as if someone had taken over this man's mind! Even if he disagreed politically, he had no reason to hate like that. It was the level of hate that someone might have if this person had murdered one of their family members. His eyes changed. I tried to change the subject and asked him if I could pray for his leg that he told me was hurting. He said yes, and so I touched him and prayed for him and even prayed that God would melt that hate away. He saw his wife and scurried off quickly!

Back to the Story of the Tower of Babel/Darkness

One of the ruling spirits we have been dealing with in this tower of darkness is the spirit of Jezebel. The spirit of Jezebel is a very controlling one, a spirit of witchcraft. Jezebel is an expert at false accusation and guilt. We read in 1 Kings 21 the story of how King Ahab wanted to buy a vineyard that the owner, Naboth, wouldn't sell to him. His wife, Jezebel, created a *false accusation* against him to have Naboth killed in order for her husband to get the vineyard. The spirit of Jezebel wants the vineyard of America and will do whatever it takes to get it. (However, God and His Church are standing in her way!) We are seeing a lot of false accusations today in high places and we need to continue to pray for this spirit to be cast down. The Bible is very clear about how God feels about false accusations and lies:

> *These six things the Lord hates,*
> *Yes, seven are an abomination to Him:*
> *A proud look,*
> *A lying tongue,*
> *Hands that shed innocent blood,*
> *A heart that devises wicked plans,*
> *Feet that are swift in running to evil,*
> *A false witness who speaks lies,*
> *And one who sows discord among brethren.*
>
> Proverbs 6:16–19

We could look at all seven attributes that are listed in the above verse and easily see every one of them played out in the kingdom of darkness on full display for us to see:

— 1. *A Proud Look*: One of the things that I believe has been so frustrating to many of us is how certain people in high positions have a sense that the same rules don't apply to them as everyone else. This attitude is one of pride, and the Bible says that pride comes before destruction. (Proverbs 16:18)

— 2. *A Lying Tongue*: Lies are meant to deceive and put people in bondage. The reason that the fake news and some liberal elites tell so many lies is so that they can get away with crimes and put in place their evil agenda. The Bible says the devil is the *father of liars* (John 8:44).

— 3. *Hands That Shed Innocent Blood*: An obvious analogy here is the push for abortion on demand. Abortion was always wrong; however, it has been shocking how they pushed the envelope to want to abort fully formed babies in the womb; that is horrible. We also know that people with dictator-like, controlling attitudes don't mind having people killed that are in their way. We have seen many suspicious deaths in the news that God will reveal the truth about.

— *4. A Heart That Devises Wicked Plans*: Okay, it is one thing when someone has a sudden sin that they do that was unplanned, but it is another thing to know what you are doing and carefully plan it. We have seen very elaborate schemes take place to steal the election from Donald Trump and those who voted for him (*2000 Mules* movie, Dinesh D'souza). We saw a fake Russian collusion narrative that was carefully planned out to take down a sitting president. After years of investigation and millions of taxpayer dollars, they could not come up with any crime that Donald Trump or his family committed.

— *5. Feet That Are Swift In Running to Evil:* The Bible says that evil company corrupts good habits (1 Corinthians 15:33). We have seen the lines drawn between good and evil like never before. People have chosen sides. It is one thing to *accidentally* find yourself joined with evil people, and it is another thing to be swift to join their side even if you know they are committing crimes and/or standing against Godly values.

— *6. A False Witness That Speaks Lies*: We have seen a lot of people who are swift to stand with evil people and even willing to commit perjury in front of courts and Congress to help their evil cause. It is never okay to falsely accuse innocent people.

— *7. One Who Sows Discord Among the Brethren*: This is the attribute that God hates the most! One of the major ways people create discord is with false accusations and lies. Lies bring confusion and unnecessary suspicion. False accusations of racism have been one of the fake news media's favorite ways to divide us. Even though, unfortunately, racism has been real in the past and present, we have seen many on the left bring false accusations of racism just because of disagreement of political views.

— A Personal Example of Witnessing False Accusation in a Church —

I personally witnessed a similar kind of accusation in a church I attended in the 80's and early 90's that I mentioned in the above explanation of *sowing discord*. The church was a multicultural congregation of several thousand people and had been for many years; we were all getting along fine as far as I knew. However, some of the leaders became embroiled in a sexual abuse scandal that became very public, and many people were leaving the church. My husband and I had not left yet, still trying to figure out if these allegations were true. However, I will never forget one day when the senior pastor claimed in front of the congregation that the people who were leaving were *racists!* I remember being startled at such a strange accusation for a church who had been taught and lived out a standard of equality for many years. In addition, I knew most of those people that were leaving, and they were *obviously* upset about the sexual immorality going on in leadership (which should be a big deal). That is just a plain false accusation. The goal of someone who makes false accusations is usually to point away from *their* sins or crimes so they can put the attention and accusation somewhere else!

The Dangers of Lies

As I said earlier, lies produce bondage because lies come from our enemy, the devil, who is the father of all lies. Lies also produce fear because you don't know who to trust.

Recently, the Lord really impressed upon me to make sure I emphasized in this book how wrong and dangerous lying is. Sometimes people put lies in different categories of "not so bad" to "really bad," but lying is wrong, and we should be lovers of truth. Since Jesus is the truth and the devil perpetrates lies, we are ultimately choosing between light and darkness:

> *Jesus said to him, "I am the way, the truth, and the life. No one comes to the Father except through Me.*
>
> John 14:6

> *You are of your father the devil, and the desires of your father you want to do. He was a murderer from the beginning, and does not stand in the truth, because there is no truth in him. When he speaks a lie, he speaks from*

> *his own resources, for he is a liar and the father of it.*
>
> John 8:44

The above two passages should be clear that *lies* fall under the kingdom of darkness. Lies are what the Tower of Babel is built on. The word "Babel" means *confusion; mixture*.[2] Think about that for a moment. The enemy builds his tower on lies that are meant to confuse people. He can deceive with the "*mixture*" part of that. He mixes some truth with the lies. Some of his worst deceptions have some truth mixed with the lies in order to confuse.

For example, the devil deceived Eve by bringing doubt and confusion to the instructions God had given them of what they could eat and what not to eat in the garden, which resulted in a terrible choice (Genesis 3:1–7). The devil also did this to Jesus in his forty days of fasting in the wilderness by misusing scriptures (Luke 4:1–13). This, of course, did not work with Jesus. Jesus *is* the truth personified!

When we continue to fellowship with someone who lies often, it is not good for our mental state of mind. For example, as I told you earlier in chapter four, a person in my life has lied about me regularly and to me regularly, but I tried countless times to turn the other cheek and be patient, loving and forgiving since this was a close relative. However, God had to deal with me and show me how it was affecting me emotionally. (My friends who love me also pointed out how it was affecting me emotionally!) Because of my sensitivity, and especially when I was not in a good state of mind, I would be tempted to believe the cutdown remarks and lies against me, and it would really mess with my confidence and emotions. I would battle heaviness and depression after these kinds of conversations.

One of the enemy's tactics to get us to believe a lie is to repeat the lie over and over. That is one reason it is dangerous to listen to news networks that have been proven to lie a lot. After a while, it is really propaganda to lead you into a path of deception. Deceptive news network propaganda is many times one of the tools used to assist dictator-type governments in keeping the people deceived and under their control. Then when the people finally figure out they have been duped, usually by that time it is hard to leave and get out of the country.

Lies are meant to give us slow indoctrination. That is why we must shun lies and run to the truth. The enemy wants us to just be accustomed to being lied to and not expect anything better. Once the fake news narrative and all the lies have been fully exposed in our nation and world, "we the people" should refuse to listen to liars anymore. Politicians and news networks that have regularly lied to us need to have no more influence in our lives. If we don't vote for them or watch their news, they will lose their positions. We need to insist on having reliable, truthful news programs that bring us facts, not ideology and lies. God does not want us to put up with lies anymore.

> *And you shall know the truth, and the truth shall make you free.*
>
> John 8:32

Truth brings liberty, and lies bring bondage. We must choose and run to the truth.

On a personal level, the devil loves to hurl insults and accusations in our minds. He is the original *"accuser of the brethren."* That is why it is important that we fill our minds with the truth in the Word concerning what God says about us.

The Tower of the Kingdom of God

> *My loving kindness and my fortress,*
> *My high **tower** and my deliverer,*
> *My shield and the One in whom I take refuge,*
> *Who subdues my people under me.* (emphasis added)
>
> Psalm 144:2

God's tower for His kingdom is one of love, power, protection, deliverance, and refuge. His tower will outlast the devil's ALWAYS. God Himself is our tower. Acts 17:28, *"for **in Him** we live and move and have our being…"* (emphasis added)

God's tower is built with a foundation of truth so it cannot fall. The truth is Jesus, and He is our Rock and secure foundation:

> *"Therefore whoever hears these sayings of Mine, and does them, I will liken him to a wise man who built his house on the rock: and the rain descended, the floods came, and the winds blew and beat on that house; and it did not fall, for it was founded on the rock. But everyone who hears these sayings of Mine, and does not do them, will be like a foolish man who built his house on the sand: and the rain descended, the floods came, and the winds blew and beat on that house; and it fell. And great was its fall."*
>
> Matthew 7:24–27

For our nation and many places on earth, we are about to see the Tower of Babel come crumbling down, and great will be its fall! However, when this happens, we will need to rebuild our nation with the proper principles of truth and Godly values. This will take all hands on deck!

— Unity of Faith is a Key to our Victory —

I believe one of the biggest keys for victory for the people of God is "*unity*." God's kind of unity is based on love and commitment to God and each other. When you think of how powerful the Tower of Babel was when they moved in unity on the dark side, could you think of how much **more powerful** our unity would be on the kingdom of God's side? The devil and his kingdom would get away with far less if we had that kind of unity!

God does not need to have all of His children in unity in order to accomplish big things and win big battles, however. Just like the story of Gideon and the three hundred, which I highlighted in chapter two of this book, God accomplished a great victory through a remnant of the nation. Yes, the rest of Israel got on board with the battle after the initial breakthrough. In fact, God can accomplish a great victory with just two people who will believe big. One example of this principle would be the story of Jonathan and his armor bearer, who had a massive victory against the Philistines just because they believed God could do anything through a few or many (1 Samuel 14:1–23). The scripture says in Leviticus 26:8, *"Five of you shall chase a hundred, and a hundred of you shall put ten thousand to flight; your enemies shall fall by the sword before you."* Therefore, although one person plus God is pretty powerful, the more people we have in unity, the greater the multiplication of God's power! The more of us that can get on the same page with God, the better.

Now, when I speak of unity in the Body of Christ, I'm not suggesting that we need to agree doctrinally on all things or all go to the same church to have unity. The real goal is that we are on the same page with God; then, we will be more and more on the same page with each other. As we all commit to seek God for truth in all areas, and ask Him to reveal any deception in our hearts and minds, then we will by default have much more agreement in important areas. Therefore, since God is always right, we want to be tuned in to the frequency of heaven!

One of the major ways in which God showed me what unity looks like in the Body of Christ is the fact that we are "*family*" and must see ourselves as family. Yes, I'm old enough to hear the song in my mind right now of the Pointer Sisters singing, "*We are family! I got all my sisters with me...*" (and brothers of course). What constitutes family in the Body of Christ is that you have made Jesus Christ your Savior. Then you have been "born again" into the *family of God*. In Ephesians 3:14–15, we read, "*For this reason I bow my knees to the Father of our Lord Jesus Christ, from whom the whole* **family** *in heaven and earth is named.*" (emphasis added)

Notice that the above verse says our family is in heaven *and* earth. Here is a scripture to further back up this:

> *Therefore we also, since we are surrounded by* **so great a cloud of witnesses,** *let us lay aside every weight, and the sin which so easily ensnares us, and let us run with endurance the race that is set before us, looking unto Jesus, the author and finisher of our faith, who for the joy that was set before Him endured the cross, despising the shame, and has sat down at the right hand of the throne of God.* (emphasis added)
>
> Hebrews 12:1–2

Our family is not only all Christians here on earth, but also the ones who have already gone to heaven. They are in a cloud of witnesses cheering us on to complete our part of the race; they have done their part of the race. They are rooting for us, and we don't want to disappoint them. We want to take the baton they passed to us and make them proud.

If you think about it, we, the Body of Christ on earth, are already spiritually living in heaven at the same time we are on earth:

> *But God, who is rich in mercy, because of His great love with which He loved us, even when we were dead in trespasses, made us alive together with Christ (by grace you have been saved), and raised us up together, and **made us sit together in the heavenly places in Christ Jesus,** that in the ages to come He might show the exceeding riches of His grace in His kindness toward us in Christ Jesus.* (emphasis added)
>
> Ephesians 2:4–7

Just like Jesus lives in all of us and also is present in heaven, we physically live here, but spiritually, we are also seated in heaven. The main difference between the family on earth and the family in heaven is that we who are on earth are *still* in the battle. We have the privilege to make a difference for the Lord here, and we want to finish our race well!

Jesus clearly expressed to His disciples that He wanted us to have love and unity like He had with His Father. Jesus's relationship with His Father and Holy Spirit is one of family. They are one, yet they have three distinct personalities and functions.

> *Now I am no longer in the world, but these are in the world, and I come to You. Holy Father, keep through Your name those whom You have given Me, that they may be one as we are.*
>
> John 17:11

> *...that they all may be one, as You, Father, are in Me, and I in You; that they also may be one in Us, that the world may believe that You sent Me. And the glory which You gave Me I have given them, that they may be one just as We are one: I in them, and You in Me; that they may be made perfect in one, and that the world may know that You have sent Me, and have loved them as You have loved Me.*
>
> John 17:21–23

In the description of the Tower of Babel in Genesis 11, we read that they *"were one and had one language."* Again, that was unity on the dark side. However, for us in the Body of Christ, I believe it means that we are members of the Body of Christ in heaven and on earth, which is fitly joined together with Jesus the head. Just like every part of a natural body has a different function yet still is one body, so do we each have a different calling and function, but we still belong to one body. As far as having one language goes, I believe that is the *language of love!* Everything we do and say should be based out of our love relationship with God and each other (1 Corinthians 13). Also, our language is that of the Holy Spirit that was poured out on God's Church on the day of Pentecost. As those disciples began to cross language barriers with the gift of tongues, God brought unity of language within His Church. This was God's divine reversal of what happened at the Tower of Babel when he confused their language.

Language of Love

The Bible says that the world will take notice when we learn to walk in love:

> *A new commandment I give to you, that you love one another; as I have loved you, that you also love one another.* **By this all will know that you are My disciples, if you have love for one another.** (emphasis added)
> John 13:34–35

This could be the key of why many in the world do not believe the gospel we preach! When we have the kind of love God is calling us to, Jesus said that ALL will know you are My disciples! Wow!

> *And now abide faith, hope, love, these three;* **but the greatest of these is love.** (emphasis added)
> 1 Corinthians 13:13

If you have love, you will have faith and hope also. However, love is probably the hardest attribute to walk in because it involves PEOPLE! You can have faith and hope that God will do amazing things for you, yet not have love for your neighbor. You can even do things for God that have selfish motives and are not born out of love. In fact, in I Corinthians 13:3 we find out that someone can give the ultimate sacrifice of martyrdom, but if their motives are wrong, well… they may not get rewarded for it!

We need all the gifts that the Holy Spirit has for us, but they need to flow out of our love for God and for each other. For example, in Galatians 5:6, we read that faith works through love. Also, the Bible says that love is a sign that you are born of God!

> *Beloved, let us love one another, for love is of God; and everyone who loves is born of God and knows God.*
>
> 1 John 4:7

I searched for the phrase *"love one another"* in Bible Gateway and came up with twenty-five of those phrases in the New Testament. I am very sure that God wants us to love one another! It was pointed out to me that five times five equals twenty-five. We know that the number five in the Bible stands for grace! Therefore, it will take a lot of grace to love one another!

Jesus warns us when He is speaking about signs of the end times in Matthew 24, that the love of many will grow cold:

> *And because lawlessness will abound, the love of many will grow cold.*
>
> Matthew 24:12

We have seen an extreme rise of lawlessness in America and around the world. The result of lawlessness in a society that disrespects the truth of God's Word is cold love. Cold love is associated with apathy because you just don't care. The lawlessness we are facing today is rooted in the Tower of Babel that confuses what is right and wrong. The world has put out the accusatory vibes of intimidation over the Church that tells us that if we tell someone the truth, we are speaking hate. But the Bible tells us that a true friend will speak the truth:

> *Faithful are the wounds of a friend,*
> *But the kisses of an enemy are deceitful.*
> Proverbs 27:6

— A Personal Testimony of Understanding Family in the Body of Christ

As I mentioned in chapter one, I was born again at the age of eighteen in a large charismatic church in a suburb of Atlanta, GA. I went forward to receive Jesus at a youth service and later joined the church. This was a precious turning point of my life; however, the bitter part was that my friends and family refused to come with me on this journey. God was faithful, and this local church quickly became my new family, and I made many new friends. However, although I learned so many things about Jesus and experienced the Holy Spirit in amazing ways at this church, there were some deep problems going on that I was not aware of. Probably because of the great success of this church, becoming well known around the world and on television, the enemy tempted the leadership of this church with pride. We began to hear messages that implied that this church was the greatest and that leaving and going anywhere else would be a downgrade or even an act of rebellion. The church began to teach an out of balance viewpoint on submitting to leadership, and my soft personality fell easy victim to this control. There were scary stories of what happened to people that left the church. I honestly felt that I would have left God if I left that church.

I remember one Sunday night driving to a service and noticing a small church on the side of the road that looked interesting and feeling this strange desire to go in there. I quickly dismissed the idea because I thought that I would be missing God to go to another church. I then drove to my church denying that desire as if I would have committed adultery on them to do so! I still wonder what would have happened if I had taken that risk to visit the other church.

After I was there about ten years and had married my wonderful husband Jim, whom I met there, the church began to go through some serious scandals. Eventually, the church began to lose many members, and my husband and I left also. It was one of the most traumatic times of my life, because I had made my relationship with God to be mainly connected with this place, and I had to learn how to find God outside of there and find another church.

However, I remember a significant moment when I looked around at other churches and realized I had a big family out there I had not met yet. I saw *all Christians* as my brothers and sisters. I still get teary eyed when I think of how wonderful it is to know that I am part of a very large, wonderful family of believers here on earth and in heaven. Even now I love relating to the whole body. I love seeing different ministers on TV and social media and watching other people's testimonies. I never get tired of that. I love how God has made all of us different with different gifts and callings, but yet together we make up the beautiful body of Christ!

──We are One Beautiful Body of Christ──

I love the scripture below because it represents the beautiful body of Christ which is made up of many different colors, races, and nationalities. The royal daughter (the Church of the Living God) will be brought to King Jesus in her robe of many colors.

> *The royal daughter is all glorious within*
>   *the palace;*
> *Her clothing is woven with gold.*
> *She shall be brought to the King in*
>   *robes of many colors;*
> *The virgins, her companions who follow her,*
>   *shall be brought to You.*
>
>   Psalm 45:13–14

We are royalty because we belong to the King of Kings and the Lord of Lords, JESUS. We are His family of kings and priests (Revelation 1:6, 5:10). Our clothing is woven in gold because gold represents righteousness in the Bible, and Jesus has made us righteous through His blood that paid for all of our sins! We are many colors like a rainbow because we are made up of every tribe, tongue, and nation (Revelation 5:9).

Here is another important scripture that shows our oneness in Him:

> *For as the body is one and has many members, but all the members of that one body, being many, are one body, so also is Christ. For by one Spirit we were all baptized into one body—whether Jews or Greeks, whether slaves or free—and have all*

> *been made to drink into one Spirit. For in fact the body is not one member but many.*
>
> 1 Corinthians 12:12–14

In Acts 4:32–35, we read how the early Church had come together and sold their possessions to distribute freely among themselves. One day, my husband, Jim, had a revelation of what *"having all things in common"* would mean for us today (Acts 4:32). He saw how we all share in the spiritual gifts of each other in the Body of Christ. No one of us works in all the gifts and callings, or we might be tempted to be proud, and we all know how that turns out; it doesn't end well (Proverbs 16:18)! However, when we make a conscious effort to *enjoy and appreciate* each other's gifts, we are all benefiting from each other's gifts:

> *There are diversities of gifts, but the same Spirit. There are differences of ministries, but the same Lord. And there are diversities of activities, but it is the same God who works all in all.* **But the manifestation of the Spirit is given to each one for the profit of all**: *for to one is given the word of wisdom through the Spirit, to another the word of knowledge through the same Spirit, to another faith by the same Spirit, to another gifts of healings by the same Spirit, to another the working of miracles, to another prophecy, to another discerning of spirits, to another different kinds of tongues, to another the interpretation of tongues. But one and the same Spirit works all these things, distributing to each one individually as He wills.* (emphasis added)
>
> 1 Corinthians 12: 4–11

All the gifts are for the *"profit of all."* For example, not all of us can sing and play instruments, yet we all have our favorite musicians and singers that we enjoy listening to. Another practical analogy would be when we have a "potluck" dinner with a group of people in which everyone brings a dish. No one wants to eat only the dish they bring; that would be boring. We all love sampling many of the different delicious dishes that others brought! Hence, God can feed us spiritually with the different gifts He has distributed in the Body of Christ. Instead of being tempted to be jealous of another's gift, instead partake and be blessed by their gift!

The Body of Christ Has Power

As the people of God, His body on earth, God has given us power to bind and to loose (Matthew 18:18). To put that in simple terms, we have the authority to allow something or not allow something. Jesus said that we are the salt of the earth. God expects His people to *believe* we are in charge "spiritually" of the place we live in. Just like you would not "allow" an intruder in your home, we need to not "allow" the devil to have his way in our nation, communities, and home. *As for me and my nation, we will serve the Lord!* Also, Jesus promises to *always* be in our midst when we gather together in His name. Therefore, we are ruling together, with Him in our midst!

> *"Again I say to you that if two of you agree on earth concerning anything that they ask, it will be done for them by My Father in heaven. For where two or three are gathered*

> *together in My name, I am there in the midst of them."*
>
> Matthew 18:19–20

As I said earlier, we are not likely going to agree on everything when it comes to how we interpret scriptures. However, we need to learn to agree on the important things. For example, since this book is about winning the battle over our nation, let me speak a few things to the Church in America. The important things I believe would be what is the obvious standard in the Word of God. It should be easy to discern many things that the Bible makes clear like sexual immoralities, abortion (murder), lying, stealing, and other moral standards of the Word. These should be easy to be on the same page about. Therefore, when we are voting, we should vote for who we think best represents our biblical values, not based on our traditions of the past but on what we best discern would be the will and values of God. If we are not sure about something, then God tells us to ask Him, and He will freely give us the wisdom we need (James 1:5). If we, God's people, in this nation just stood together on biblical values, then the enemy would lose ground quickly in a lot of areas. It would be game over!

If we learn to recognize each other as "family" just because of our faith in Jesus, then that would take care of a lot of things when it comes to disunity. When you think of a natural family with several siblings, you can see that one day they grow up and have separate families and live in different locations. They probably have different viewpoints on a lot of things, but when they come together for a family reunion, they are family! We can do this in the Body of Christ! Jesus wouldn't ask us to do something that is not possible.

──Maturity is Related to Understanding We are Family──

God never meant for us to be so divided. Paul admonished the Corinthian church for such divisions and called them "carnal" for doing so.

> *Now I say this, that each of you says, "I am of Paul," or "I am of Apollos," or "I am of Cephas," or "I am of Christ."*
>
> 1 Corinthians 1:12
>
> *For when one says, "I am of Paul," and another, "I am of Apollos,"* **are you not carnal***?*
>
> *Who then is Paul, and who is Apollos, but ministers through whom you believed, as the Lord gave to each one? I planted, Apollos watered, but God gave the increase. So then neither he who plants is anything, nor he who waters, but God who gives the increase.* (emphasis added)
>
> 1 Corinthians 3:4–7

Here is the definition of the word "carnal"[3]:

— *pertaining to or characterized by the flesh or the body, its passions and appetites; sensual: carnal pleasures*

— *not spiritual; merely human; temporal; worldly: a man of secular, rather carnal, leanings.*

In other words, being carnal is immaturity. It is of the flesh—not spiritual. The context in which Paul exhorted the Corinthians to not be carnal was that they were calling themselves followers of certain leaders, rather than followers of Jesus first. Let me explain how I believe this translates to the Church world today. Obviously, because of location and also personal callings we are going to attend different churches and follow different leaders. However, in our mind and how we relate to the Body of Christ, we must always see Jesus as our head FIRST. All of the other five-fold ministries listed in Ephesians 4:11 are there to equip us for the work of the ministry. We should honor their gifts and treat our leaders with respect because they are a gift from God to us. Another way of looking at it is that spiritual leaders are like spiritual parents and there should be a type of honor like we honor our natural parents. However, we must see ourselves as belonging to Jesus first and everybody and everything else second. We must see all of those who have made Jesus their Savior as our brothers and sisters. Jesus is our husband. We are the Bride of Christ. The Church is our family—one family! We are truly brothers and sisters.

> *For this reason I bow my knees to the Father of our Lord Jesus Christ, from whom the whole family in heaven and earth is named…*
> Ephesians 3:14–15

One day, as I was thinking about the fact that we are having such disunity in America right now, this thought came to my mind: AS THE CHURCH GOES, SO GOES THE NATION. We are the example. We can't expect the world to get along if we don't.

There are some people, however, who we will never be in unity with, nor should we.

> *Do not be unequally yoked together with unbelievers. For what fellowship has righteousness with lawlessness? And what communion has light with darkness?*
>
> 2 Corinthians 6:14

We want to love and be a witness to everyone. However, some people we can't hang around because we don't want that darkness on us!

A political example (that is my personal opinion) is that many on the left have chosen darkness, and it would be impossible to get along with them unless they turn to God. I'm only guessing, but I believe President Trump had thought he could get along with the Democrats and bring unity to both parties since he had supported both Democrats and Republicans in the past; however, things had gotten to the place that no matter how hard he tried, the Democrats were going to resist. It doesn't matter if it was things they were for in the past like helping minorities or building the wall: if they were not going to get the credit, they were now not for it. Many of the Democrats simply became more and more on the side of darkness, with antichrist agendas and their false accusations and unwillingness to do what was best for the country. I'm convinced that they would have shot their feet to get even with their toes, just so they could have the final say! This reminds me of a scripture in Matthew:

> *But to what shall I liken this generation? It is like children sitting in the marketplaces and calling to their companions, and saying:*
> > *"We played the flute for you,*
> > *And you did not dance;*
> > *We mourned to you,*
> > *And you did not lament."*

> *For John came neither eating nor drinking, and they say, "He has a demon." The Son of Man came eating and drinking, and they say, "Look, a glutton and a winebibber, a friend of tax collectors and sinners!" But wisdom is justified by her children.*
>
> Matthew 11:16–19

Obviously, Jesus was pointing out the hypocrisy of the Pharisees. They complained that John lived a strange, secluded lifestyle in the desert, not eating and drinking like the rest or attending their parties. Then Jesus came along and was eating and drinking with the people, attending weddings and parties, and they criticized him over that. The point here is that when people decide they are not going to like you, they will criticize you no matter what. The Pharisees criticized anybody they felt threatened their control over people. It was all about their position!

I was definitely praying for unity for both parties for a while; however, that changed when one day I had a vision of a line being drawn between the left and the right because of the dark agenda that many on the left had chosen. However, even though the Republicans stood for many of our Christian values, many of them were found swimming in the swamp also. I do believe though that as darkness and lies continue to be exposed, then we as a nation will have greater unity because of truth being revealed. The choice will not necessarily be between Democrats and Republicans, but between truth and lies, and darkness and light. I believe the citizens of America will become more united as the fog of war is lifted and it becomes clear what is true and what is a lie.

Let's dream a little: Maybe one day we won't need any parties in America; there will be general elections held that are not attached to a party where we choose people based on their character and beliefs. Dreaming even bigger, I want to see a Congress and Senate that pray together and vote on bills. I know that is a stretch; however, all things are possible with God!

In Closing

True unity only works when we are first in unity with God. God's way is always the right way! When it comes to the Church, we need to accept the simple fact that we are family. I believe the principles in this book will MAKE THE CHURCH GREAT AGAIN as well as MAKE AMERICA GREAT AGAIN. The Church is the salt of the earth and should understand how important our role is!

As far as unity in America goes, we need a return to patriotism. We need to recognize each other as citizens of America! I believe the disunity that has been stirred up has been the result of many lies, deceptions, and false accusations. We are in the season of the *great reveal*! God is revealing truth and exposing darkness. I believe most Americans will be on the same page when the fog of lies lifts and we can all see clearly who are the good guys and who are the bad guys.

THE DAY OF THE PROPHETS
The Showdown at Mt. Carmel
Chapter 9

> *Surely the Lord God does nothing, unless He reveals His secret to His servants the prophets.*
> Amos 3:7

I have always loved and honored the people who have prophetic giftings. I never get tired of having someone prophesy a message to me from God, especially when I know there is no way they could have known about that situation in my life. I love it when God encourages and gives us hope through prophetic messages in our personal lives. It is exciting also to have someone confirm and encourage you in what you know your callings and giftings are. We know how the devil loves to bring doubt to our minds when we have heard from God about something He has called us to do. We often hear the enemy's whiny voice say, *"Has God said?"* The devil still throws that same fiery *doubt dart* that he used on Eve in the garden! When someone prophesies what you feel you have already been shown by God for your life, it builds the necessary confidence and confirmation you need to help anchor your faith in times of doubt and warfare.

The encouragement from prophetic words given to me personally has greatly helped in the writing of this book. This being the first book I have ever written, there was a lot of insecurity, along with a lot of warfare. People prophesied words to me about my call to write that knew nothing or very little about me. That has helped anchor me on the days of doubt and discouragement.

In this chapter, however, I'm going to discuss the importance of prophecy when it comes to national affairs. God has always had prophets to speak to the kings and the people in both Old Testament times and New Testament times concerning their nation and the battles they were facing. He is still the same today, providing prophets to the Body of Christ to give us insight into what God is doing in our current culture. There are many well-known and trusted prophets in the Body of Christ that have prophesied concerning Donald Trump's governmental assignment during this time in history along with many other issues our nation and world are facing. God does not want His people to be clueless; He wants us to have heaven's perspective in the midst of trying times!

I'm not saying that we blindly listen to everyone who says they have a word from God. The Bible says in 1 John 4:1, *"Beloved, do not believe every spirit, but test the spirits, whether they are of God; because many false prophets have gone out into the world."* Here are a few ways we can test the spirits:

— Does this prophet have a proven track record of fulfilled prophecies? Most people have accidentally missed God before; however, if someone is a true prophet, they will get it right most of the time. Also, remember to give the prophecy time to be fulfilled. Many times prophets get words from God years ahead of time.

— Prophecies should not violate the standards of the Bible. For example, if someone prophesied that God is okay with abortion, then you would know that is not from God because the Bible is clear that we should not murder and that life comes from God and is precious (Psalm 139:13).

— Prophecies you are hearing in public will many times confirm what you are getting in your personal prayer times. For example, when I began to hear men and women of God prophecy that Donald Trump was being called to the presidency at this time in history, I could easily agree because God had told me the same thing. If the prophecy is not something you have gotten in prayer already, then you can ask God to confirm that to you.

— Jesus said that His sheep knows His voice (John 10:27). Therefore, when we have been spending time with God and His Word, we will recognize His voice when He speaks through others. Usually I have a "knowing" on the inside of me that I just heard truth.

— Having a lack of peace in your spirit or even a feeling of fear can be red flags. Even if God is warning His people about something serious that will happen, He will always give His people hope and promise of His love and protection over us (Psalm 91). We can still

> live in the land of Goshen when the world is getting plagues. (However, if the prophecy is a warning to the wicked of coming judgment if they don't repent, then they should feel a little fear and get right with God!)

Jesus has given five major different leadership callings in the Body of Christ to equip the saints. We call this the five-fold ministry. They are all equally important: however, at certain times and seasons, one calling may be emphasized more than another.

> *And He Himself gave some to be apostles, some prophets, some evangelists, and some pastors and teachers, for the equipping of the saints for the work of ministry, for the edifying of the body of Christ*
>
> Ephesians 4:11–12

Because of the intensity of the warfare of these times we are in, we have been in a season where the prophetic has been at the forefront. We have been in an Elijah moment where it has been necessary to confront the prophets of Baal, along with Jezebel and many other demonic strongholds. Prophets in the Body of Christ are generally very bold individuals; it takes boldness to confront Jezebel and her crew. It takes boldness to step out and take the risk of prophesying to individuals or nations. Sometimes the prophetic has been misunderstood in the Church because, unfortunately, the devil has at times sown the tares among the wheat, resulting in false prophecies. However, we should not throw the baby out with the bathwater! God still has five leadership callings in His Church, and we need all five. We can seek God and test the prophecies as I outlined above.

I have personally found it very comforting—as I'm sure many of you have also—how God has given us so many encouraging words of His good plan for this nation during this harsh season we have been in. Many people are having dreams, visions, and prophetic words over America that God will come through and bring about a great victory for this nation. I personally have fed myself regularly on the Elijah List Ministries[1] and Elijah Streams videos (Rumble and Facebook), where Steve Shultz has given a platform for the prophets to reveal what they are being shown.

I would like to emphasize again, as I did in an earlier chapter, that we can all prophesy. There are individuals that move in the office of the Prophet (five-fold ministry), which would mean that it is their primary call and that they would be usually the ones to speak to kings (government leaders) and be a major voice to the Body of Christ. However, we are His sheep, and we all hear His voice for ourselves and can also hear for others. Therefore, believe God to speak to you and through you. One day I heard this phrase in my mind: *a nation of prophets*. I believe God is expanding the prophetic at this time in history!

The Showdown at Mount Carmel

In this section I'm going to highlight the story of when Elijah confronted the prophets of Baal in Israel. I will also show how we are reliving this story currently in this nation!

This story begins with King Ahab reigning in Israel (1 Kings 16-22). The Bible says that he did more evil than all the kings before him, which included taking Jezebel as his wife, the daughter of the king of the Sidonians, and serving Baal. Israel knew that any form of idolatry was a grave sin against

God. Baal worship sometimes included ritual prostitution and even child sacrifice (Jeremiah 19:5). God raised up prophets during this time to confront these evils, with the major prophet being Elijah. In today's terms, Baal worship would include sexual immoralities and abortion.

The first mention of Elijah is in 1 Kings 17:1, *"And Elijah the Tishbite, of the inhabitants of Gilead, said to Ahab, 'As the Lord God of Israel lives, before whom I stand, there shall not be dew nor rain these years, except at my word.'"* Elijah was sent to Ahab to show that God was going to withhold national blessings like rain, which they needed to grow food and have water, because of these wicked practices.

During this time, Ahab's wife, Jezebel, was killing the prophets. Thankfully, a man named Obadiah, who feared God and ran Ahab's household, had hidden from Jezebel one hundred of the prophets in two caves. Jezebel in this story, similarly to the people who operate in this spirit today, hates the prophets of God because of the power of God they walk in.

In this story in 1 Kings 18, we read how Elijah called together the four hundred and fifty prophets of Baal on Mount Carmel with all of Israel gathered together and watching. Elijah said to the people of Israel, *"How long will you falter between two opinions? If the Lord is God, follow Him; but if Baal, follow him."* He told the prophets of Baal to prepare a sacrifice without the fire and that he would do the same. The God who answers by fire is the one true God. Of course, we know that our God, the one true God, answered by fire, and Elijah then executed all the prophets of Baal.

In America today, we have for sure been in a similar fight between good and evil. It has been clear that there are many on the left who would love to shut the voice of the Church and put us in a corner somewhere in timeout! What the Church knows to be truth and the moral standard taught in the Bible is what some on the liberal left call "hate speech." This would be similar to Jezebel killing the prophets. The spirit of Jezebel does not want the voice of the Church to remain. The attack on our children through abortion and immoral indoctrination in our schools is a form of "Baal worship." The enemy is after our children, and we have to make a stand for them.

We have seen a division in our country like never before. We want unity; however, we want unity on the Lord's side. Therefore, there has been a choosing of sides, just like when Elijah told the people of Israel to choose whether they were going to follow God or Baal. I remember one day having a vision of the Capitol building in Washington, D.C.—the government leaders were choosing sides between darkness and light. On one hand, the division has been painful; on the other hand, it makes it much easier to see who is on God's side and agree with them!

Also, we have seen the public display of demonic spirits in a much bolder way than we have seen in our country in the past. When the witches were publicly praying against Donald Trump and trying to cast spells on him[2], we knew that we were not living in "Mayberry" anymore; this was war. Thankfully, just like in the story of Moses and Aaron confronting Pharaoh, Aaron's snake swallowed up their snake. Our God is always more powerful. The Bible says in 1 John 4:4, *"You are of God, little children, and have overcome them, because He who is in you is greater than he who is in the world."* The Church has been in prayer for our nation, and God will win!

I found it interesting in the story of Elijah that he prophesied to King Ahab that there would not be rain except at his word. That is boldness and courage! God loves it when His people trust His voice enough to stand before kings and make bold declarations like that. And yes, they were in drought until after the Mount Carmel showdown. I thought it was very interesting that immediately after it says that Elijah executed the prophets of Baal, the passage says:

> *Then Elijah said to Ahab, "Go up, eat and drink; for there is the sound of abundance of rain." So Ahab went up to eat and drink. And Elijah went up to the top of Carmel; then he bowed down on the ground, and put his face between his knees, and said to his servant, "Go up now, look toward the sea."*
>
> *So he went up and looked, and said, "There is nothing." And seven times he said, "Go again."*
>
> *Then it came to pass the seventh time, that he said, "There is a cloud, as small as a man's hand, rising out of the sea!" So he said, "Go up, say to Ahab, 'Prepare your chariot, and go down before the rain stops you.' "*
>
> *Now it happened in the meantime that the sky became black with clouds and wind, and there was a heavy rain. So Ahab rode away and went to Jezreel. Then the hand of the Lord came upon Elijah; and he girded up his loins and ran ahead of Ahab to the entrance of Jezreel.*
>
> 1 Kings 18:41–46

Prophet Elijah stood up and defeated the false prophets of Baal, and *then the rain came*. I immediately saw the prophetic significance to where we are in our nation. When the demonic in this country and evil rulers are dealt with, then the rain is coming. Many prophets have prophesied that God is going to bring justice to the evil; many will go to jail. The rain will be for us a mighty outpouring of God's Spirit and harvest in our country. This is good news!

── The Battle Against the Spirit of Jezebel

Our battle is not any different than what Elijah and Israel faced. You see, America has been on the frontline of standing for righteousness and promoting the gospel, and we have been in the devil's way of having his desire of a one-world government rule. God, however, is doing the opposite and removing the corruption we have endured. God wants to raise America up even better than we could ever imagine to promote the gospel and be a blessing to the world.

Here are some of the characteristics of the spirit of Jezebel. Jezebel uses control, witchcraft, and seduction to bring people under her rule. Jezebel brings people into idolatry, worshiping false gods. Even though the person of Jezebel in the story of Elijah was a woman, the Jezebel spirit works in both male and female. The spirit of Jezebel is a very strong spirit that even made the Prophet Elijah run for his life:

> *And Ahab told Jezebel all that Elijah had done, also how he had executed all the prophets with the sword. Then Jezebel sent a messenger to Elijah, saying, "So let the gods do to me, and more also, if I do not make your life as the life of one of them by tomorrow about this time." And when he saw that, he arose and ran for his life, and went to Beersheba, which belongs to Judah, and left his servant there.*
>
> *But he himself went a day's journey into the wilderness, and came and sat down under a broom tree. And he prayed that he might die, and said, "It is enough! Now, Lord, take my life, for I am no better than my fathers!"*
>
> 1 Kings 19:1–4

Let's put this in perspective. Elijah had just had a huge victory at Mount Carmel. Not only did God do a miracle for him by sending down fire from heaven to consume the sacrifice, but then Elijah executed all four hundred and fifty prophets of Baal. I would think Elijah would be feeling pretty good after all that. However, after Jezebel threatened to kill him, he ran for his life. The scriptures above show that Elijah became discouraged and depressed and wanted to die! This is an example of the strength of that spirit. Therefore, the spirit of Jezebel can cause those under her influence to feel fear, depression, and discouragement.

Jezebel can also be seductive. Yes, this can be sexual seduction, but the seduction also can be ideological or anything that seduces you away from our true God. In today's world, we have seen this spirit operate with the push for sexual immorality along with the deceptive ideology that just about everything goes as long as it feels good to that person. We know that is not true, that God has a standard for that in His Word. The "woke" ideology of today that pushes immoral standards even for kids is associated with Jezebel.

Jezebel wants to kill the prophets of today also. Jezebel hates those who speak truth and stand up to her evil ways. This spirit wants to cancel their voices. There have been many Christian voices censored or canceled on social media, especially the prophetic voices. Prophets are on Jezebel's hit list just like in biblical times.

We have all probably brushed up against this demon at one time or another. Anybody in your life that has tried to manipulate and control you, silence you, intimidate you, or pressure you to do things you don't want to do is probably operating in this spirit. If you have battled depression, discouragement, and fear, you probably need to get with God and see if there are any relationships that need to go!

—— Pharisees, Herod, and Antichrist Spirits

Another spirit we are dealing with today is the Pharisee spirit. Pharisees pretend to be religious and care about people, but they only really care about their control and power. They will do whatever they have to do to keep their control, even if it means to destroy someone's reputation or life. The Pharisees of Jesus's day were the leaders of the synagogues who pretended to be on the side of God, yet Jesus told the Pharisees that their father was the devil (John 8:44). The Pharisees were very accusatory to Jesus—always finding fault. If Jesus healed someone on the Sabbath, they would accuse him of working on the Sabbath instead of being happy for one of their synagogue members for being healed of a major illness or infirmity. It was the Pharisees that eventually put Jesus on the cross because of their hate for Him.

Yes, Pharisees can be in the Church, but we have seen a lot of them in political positions too! In current times, this reminds me of how the leaders of the Democratic Party and other swampy politicians treated Donald Trump. No worries—I'm not comparing Donald Trump with Jesus; however, I am comparing some of the Liberal Left with the Pharisees. (Jesus was the only perfect person and the rest of us need Jesus to be our Savior!) One thing that has really stood out in my mind to this day is the first State of the Union address that Donald Trump gave. In one year's time, he had accomplished more good than any other president in my lifetime had done in such a short time. As they celebrated how well the economy was going, with the lowest unemployment percentage in a long time, how well the minority communities had been helped, the building up of our military, and many other amazing accomplishments, I was shocked and saddened when I saw the majority of the Democratic Party leaders looking sour and sitting in their seats while the rest of the crowd was standing. These were accomplishments that helped *everybody* no matter what party affiliation they had. However, the Pharisee spirit is angry when they are not in charge and don't get credit for it!

As I said earlier, the Pharisees are very accusatory. Most of the time, people who purposely falsely accuse others end up being guilty of what they accuse or even of something worse. Have you ever seen a president have to endure so much false accusation? One false accusation after another, and it is still going on. The Pharisee spirit has a lot of hate—enough hate to want to destroy anyone or anything that they feel threatened by. That spirit has not only gone after Trump, but many of those associated with him. The Pharisee spirit is a very jealous spirit, and the Bible says that jealousy is as cruel as the grave (Song of Solomon 8:6).

The Pharisees have positioned themselves to be "gatekeepers." They decide who gets to stay and who doesn't. The Pharisees would kick people out of the synagogue for following Jesus. We can get kicked out of the social media synagogue these days also!

> *But woe to you, scribes and Pharisees, hypocrites! For you shut up the kingdom of heaven against men; for you neither go in yourselves, nor do you allow those who are entering to go in.*
>
> Matthew 23:13

Another buddy of the Pharisee and Jezebel spirits is the spirit of Herod, which is a political spirit that has a dictator flavor. Herod was a governmental leader during the time of Jesus. When the wise men visited Herod looking for Jesus, born king of the Jews, Herod believed his position was threatened and killed all the babies in that region of the ages of two and under (Matthew 2:16). The spirit of Herod is similar to the others that will do whatever is necessary to keep their position. We see the spirit of Herod working today when people will destroy their own people in order to stay in power. In the Bible, God judged and killed Herod when he allowed the people to worship him as a god:

> *So on a set day Herod, arrayed in royal apparel, sat on his throne and gave an oration to them. And the people kept shouting, 'The voice of a god and not of a man!" Then immediately an angel of the Lord struck him, because he did not give glory to God. And he was eaten by worms and died.*
>
> Acts 12:21–23

The Antichrist spirit is intertwined with all these other demonic strongholds. Antichrist is just what it says—*anti* (against) *Christ*. That spirit denies that Jesus is Lord and wants to remove Jesus from our culture. The taking down of nativity scenes and taking prayer out of schools, all in wanting to remove God out of our society, is antichrist in nature:

> *…and every spirit that does not confess that Jesus Christ has come in the flesh is not of God. And this is the spirit of the Antichrist, which you have heard was coming, and is now already in the world.*
>
> 1 John 4:3

> *Who is a liar but he who denies that Jesus is the Christ? He is antichrist who denies the Father and the Son.*
>
> 1 John 2:22

Even though the battle against us has been daunting, just remember that the Bible says in 1 John 4:4, *"...He who is in you is greater than he who is in the world."*

In Summary

The Bible makes it clear that our real enemies are not people, but principalities and powers. Yes, they work through people, but we should pray for the people that carry these spirits to be saved and set free.

> *For we do not wrestle against flesh and blood, but against principalities, against powers, against the rulers of the darkness of this age, against spiritual hosts of wickedness in the heavenly place.*
>
> Ephesians 6:12

This is a day of great boldness because of the spiritual battles we have been facing. I love the song by Robin Mark called *"Days of Elijah,"* written in 1994. Here are some of the lyrics to his song that is prophetic for where we are today:

> *These are the days of Elijah*
> *Declaring the word of the Lord*
> *And these are the days of Your servant Moses*
> *Righteousness being restored*
>
> *And though these are days of great trial*
> *Of famine and darkness and sword*

Still, we are the voice in the desert crying
"Prepare ye the way of the Lord!"

Behold, He comes riding on the clouds
Shining like the sun at the trumpet call
Lift your voice, the year of jubilee
And out of Zion's hill, salvation comes

And these are the days of Ezekiel
The dry bones becoming as flesh
And these are the days of Your servant David
Rebuilding a temple of praise

Oh, these are the days of the harvest
For the fields are as white in Your world
And we are the laborers in Your vineyard
Declaring the word of the Lord!

Behold, He comes, riding on the clouds
Shining like the sun at the trumpet call
Lift your voice, the year of jubilee
And out of Zion's hill, salvation comes

These are days of the Church, walking in great power and glory. These are the days of the prophets, declaring God's word over our nation. These are the days of the latter rain, bringing great revival to our nation and our world! These are the days of great reformation and revival! Our best days are yet to come!

Riding on the Mountaintops with Jesus
Chapter 10

> *And the Lord will make you the head and not the tail; you shall be above only, and not be beneath, if you heed the commandments of the Lord your God, which I command you today, and are careful to observe them.*
>
> Deuteronomy 28:13

The Head and **Not** the Tail

When I was nearing the delivery of our firstborn daughter, Ashley Rose, back in 1995, the doctors discovered she was breach (sitting up) through an ultrasound. They scheduled me for a procedure at the hospital where they try to turn the baby to be in the head down position for delivery. Before I went, I took it to prayer at our church. They gathered around me at the altar to pray for Ashley to turn before delivery, and my close friend, who I considered to be my spiritual mom, Judy, began to laugh and prophesy, *"She is not breach, she is the head and not the tail!"* To be honest, I didn't know what to think. Does this mean she has already turned, or will turn later? As it went, they could not turn her at the hospital and scheduled me for a C-section on February 16th. On the day of the scheduled C-section, one of the midwives had an idea to try to turn her one more time since they had already given me an epidural and my body would be relaxed. I agreed since I was not very excited about having a C-section. It worked and she was turned. Then they moved me to a hospital room and they tried to induce labor *for days* without it working, until Tuesday, the 21st, when labor finally kicked in. But guess what? She was such a big baby (9 lbs, 5 ounces), she got stuck in the birth canal and I had to have an emergency C-section anyway! Ashley truly was the head and not the tail! The Lord continued to reveal to my friend and I that Ashley was symbolic of the generation that would walk in the authority of being the "head and not the tail" like the scripture above.

In the garden of Eden, man was given dominion over the earth. Man was created to rule with God; we were made in the image of God Himself (Genesis 1:26–28). However, the devil wanted that rulership, and he deceived Adam and Eve into giving their authority to him. Fast forward to the cross, and Jesus took that authority back for us (Matthew 28:18).

After Jesus was baptized by his cousin, John the Baptist, in the Jordan River, He was led by the Holy Spirit into the wilderness to be tempted by the devil for forty days. One of the temptations the devil put before Jesus was that rulership that he took from Adam and Eve in the garden:

> *Then the devil, taking Him up on a high mountain, showed Him all the kingdoms of*

> *the world in a moment of time. And the devil said to Him, "All this authority I will give You, and their glory; for this has been delivered to me, and I give it to whomever I wish. Therefore, if You will worship before me, all will be Yours."*
>
> *And Jesus answered and said to him, "Get behind Me, Satan! For it is written, 'You shall worship the Lord your God, and Him only you shall serve.'"*
>
> Luke 4:5–8

The devil is full of pride and deceit. It is true that he took authority from Adam and Eve, thus resulting in the fall of mankind, but he never took it from God. An example of this is when Daniel was interpreting King Nebuchadnezzar's dream in Daniel 2:37, *"You, O king, are a king of kings. For the God of heaven has given you a kingdom, power, strength, and glory."* Notice that the **God of heaven** gave King Nebuchadnezzar his kingdom, not the devil, and this was before the cross. The devil is a liar and would have never kept that promise to Jesus or anyone else for that matter. It still belonged to God, and now Jesus would go to the cross and pay the price for our sins so *our authority* would be *restored* back to us and the curse be reversed *in our lives*!

> *Then He called His twelve disciples together and gave them power and authority over all demons, and to cure diseases.*
>
> Luke 9:1

When Jesus went to the cross, He defeated principalities and powers! The Lion of the Tribe of Judah prevails:

> *Having disarmed principalities and powers, He made a public spectacle of them, triumphing over them in it.*
>
> Colossians 2:15

What are the kingdoms of this world and why is it important who has authority over them? There are very good teachings out there on the seven mountains of culture: **Religion (Church), Education, Family, Business, Government, Arts & Entertainment, and Media.** Johnny Enlow (restore7.org) and Lance Wallnau (lancewallnau.com) are two ministers that my husband and I have received great teaching from concerning this. To give my own quick summary of what I have learned: ministry is in every area of life for the believer. Many times we have thought that only having a leadership or volunteer position in a local church counted as being in ministry. However, that is only one of the mountains that God wants us to use our giftings in. Every area of culture is a place for us to arise and shine for the Lord! If we are a business owner or employee, God wants our business to be a place where we can use our giftings, believing God for favor to influence that environment with Godly values. We can pray and believe for opportunities to minister to our co-workers. We can make the world a better place and shine our lights for God by our business products being made with excellence and our business dealings done with integrity. If we are in the entertainment industry, then it is an opportunity to use our creativity to influence culture with Godly values rather than promote sinful lifestyles that influence our children in the wrong way. For myself, I have had the privilege of being a stay-at-home mom, and I was aware that my children were my main ministry; this would be an example of the family mountain. However, whether you are a homemaker or have a full-time job, instilling Godly values into our families is a huge priority. Joseph, Daniel, Mordecai, and Esther are all biblical examples of making a Godly difference in the government mountain; they all four received high governmental positions in secular kingdoms, yet they did not compromise their Godly values, instead bringing about great and positive changes in their spheres of influence. On the education mountain, we want our children taught Godly values along with pro-American values of liberty. Therefore, it is super important that teachers and educators see the importance of their calling to be a Godly influence on our youth. The media mountain is super important right now with the rise of fake and deceptive news. Christians in the news industry with a gift of journalism need to use their voices to be honest news sources. In summary, we should allow the Lord to give us faith and clarity to "take these mountains" for the Lord! After all, we are supposed to rule with God!

The reason it is important for us to have authority over these mountains is that whoever has rulership in these mountains of culture influences that area either with good or evil. For example, we have seen what people who are ungodly have done to the education of our children, introducing immoral teachings that do not glorify God or our country, with socialistic values intertwined. We have seen what happens when we have a president who doesn't honor God or put America first. It results in a failed economy, chaos at our borders, and crime on the rise. We have seen what it is like when those in charge of media are perpetuating fake news and no longer publish the truth. This has resulted in deception and confusion to many. These mountains can be used for evil when in the wrong hands or be a blessing when they are in the hands of righteous people. Therefore, it is our privilege to serve God and people on these mountains. If we know we are called to a certain mountain, then we need to believe for favor to have a key position to bring positive, Godly change to that area of culture. Remember that we are the salt of the earth

(Matthew 5:13). We provide the flavor, and we don't want the enemy's flavor!

—— An Explanation of the Name of this Chapter ——

I originally had called this chapter *"Taking the Mountains."* Then, one day, I had this strong desire to call it *"Riding the Top of the Mountains."* I really wasn't sure why I wanted to call it that, but I felt drawn to that name, so I went with it. However, later during the editing process, I thought about it with my *mind of reason* and thought, "Why would I say the word 'ride'—ride on what?" Therefore, I changed it back to the original. Then one day, as I was continuing my editing process, I happened to hear an Elijah Streams broadcast aired on October 25th, 2022, where minister and author Donna Rigney told about a vision she had in church: She saw Jesus *riding* on a white horse, taking the seven mountains of culture (as I listed in the above section), and with Him were the saints in heaven and on earth *riding* on white horses with Him![1] Then I understood why I felt led to use the word "ride" in the title. Thus, I settled on the above title after this amazing confirmation and further revelation. We are riding with Jesus on white horses, taking the mountains back for the Kingdom of God! Yay God!!!

> *Now I saw heaven opened, and behold, a white horse. And He who sat on him was called Faithful and True, and in righteousness He judges and makes war. His eyes were like a flame of fire, and on His head were many crowns. He had a name written that no one*

> *knew except Himself. He was clothed with a robe dipped in blood, and His name is called The Word of God. And the armies in heaven, clothed in fine linen, white and clean, followed Him on white horses. Now out of His mouth goes a sharp sword, that with it He should strike the nations. And He Himself will rule them with a rod of iron. He Himself treads the winepress of the fierceness and wrath of Almighty God. And He has on His robe and on His thigh a name written:*
>
> KING OF KINGS
AND LORD OF LORDS.
>
> Revelation 19:11–16

The Taking Back of our Nation

I completely believe that the prayers of the saints are going to be answered for America and that we are going to get our country back and have great revival. However, we need to keep our country this time in the way we want to have it. We as Christians should want there to be a biblical worldview and Godly values in every area of society. We want our nation to flourish and have God's blessings raining down on us. We want our children to be taught by the Lord, not the devil.

> *When the righteous are in authority,*
>   *the people rejoice;*
> *But when a wicked man rules, the people groan.*
>
> Proverbs 29:2

It really does matter who is in charge. Authority figures in government and every sphere of life open doors to blessings or curses. You really can't separate what someone's core values are to how they will do their job. I find it interesting how in 1 Kings, 2 Kings, and 2 Chronicles, when you read about each king that ruled Israel or Judah, it usually begins with either *"he did evil in the sight of the Lord,"* or *"he did what was right in the sight of the Lord."* Usually, this resulted in many of the people following the king's lead of worshiping God or false idols. Again, it really does make a difference who is in charge. Therefore, we want righteous people in charge who carry the wisdom of God!

President Trump will be restored to his rightful position (if not already when you read this book), because I totally believe he rightfully won and was chosen for this time in history. However, he cannot do this battle alone even when he is back. He will need all of us to take our places in society and be the salt and light for God. These are truly going to be exciting times!

—— Having the Courage of Caleb and Joshua to Take the Land ——

Our youngest son, Kaleb Joshua, was born in 2003. When he was born, I remember the midwife proclaiming 'Kaleb Joshua – taking the land.' Of course, I loved hearing that! We had named our son after the two men of faith in the Bible, Caleb and Joshua. We had changed the "C" in Caleb to a "K" for the Kingdom of God, but also because we had a hamster named Caleb and needed to change something for our son (seriously, not joking)! However, it turned out to be a God inspired idea to spell Kaleb with a "K," because one day a couple of months after Kaleb was born, I realized that the first letters of our children's names in their birth order spelled ARK: **A**shley, **R**ebecca, and **K**aleb. Pretty cool! I did not plan that, but God did!

I remember one day a few years ago thinking and praying about how God purposely made an acronym out of the first letters of our children's names and wondering if there was anything prophetic or significant about that. What came to my mind was that in the story of Noah's Ark, God was providing a safe place for His people while He was judging the wicked on the earth, so God could do a divine "reset" with a Godly family. At first, I thought maybe that meant the "rapture" would take place in my kids' generation; however, since then I believe it means a reset for what is taking place *now* in our country and around the world. We are seeing wicked and deep state corruption exposed, and God is going to remove them from their positions. The "reset" is going to be God's reset for His children. This reset is going to bring a divine flip where the saints are going to truly be the head and not the tail!

I love the story of Caleb and Joshua in the Bible. In Numbers 13, we read how Moses sent twelve spies to spy out the land of Canaan that God had promised them. There was a man from each of the twelve tribes of Israel represented. When they came back to give their report to the children of Israel they told them that the land was truly flowing with milk and honey and showed them the amazing fruit they brought back, BUT they also told them how the descendants of Anak (giants) lived there. Immediately, Caleb spoke up:

> *Then Caleb quieted the people before Moses, and said, "Let us go up at once and take possession, for we are well able to overcome it.*
>
> Numbers 13:30

The story goes on to tell of how ten of the spies told the people they would not be able to take the land because of the giants, but Caleb and Joshua both stood with the Lord and His promises. The result of this negative news by the ten was that the children of Israel believed the bad report instead of the good. They apparently tuned into the "fake news networks" filled with doom and gloom about how the giant called *"Climate Change"* fed from the pollution created from our cars and planes (and even cows) was going to kill the planet and we would all die! (Just a little humor here.)

Joshua and Caleb continued to try to reason with their brethren to believe and trust God that He would give them victory over their enemies as promised:

> *…and they spoke to all the congregation of the children of Israel, saying: "The land we passed through to spy out is an exceedingly good land. If the Lord delights in us, then He will bring us into this land and give it to us, 'a land which flows with milk and honey.' Only do not rebel against the Lord, nor fear the people of the land, for they are our bread; their protection has departed from them, and the Lord is with us. Do not fear them."*
>
> Numbers 14:7–9

In this story, they would not listen to the good news; they chose the bad news. Have you ever noticed how it is much easier to believe the negative than the positive? This reminds me of this scripture in Philippians that encourages us to purposely meditate on the positive:

> *Finally, brethren, whatever things are true, whatever things are noble, whatever things*

> *are just, whatever things are pure, whatever things are lovely, whatever things are of good report, if there is any virtue and if there is anything praiseworthy—meditate on these things. The things which you learned and received and heard and saw in me, these do, and the God of peace will be with you.*
>
> Philippians 4:8–9

As the story continues in Numbers 14, God was angry with the children of Israel and decided to punish them by letting them wander in the wilderness forty more years until that generation of the unbelieving and faithless group died out. However, Joshua and Caleb were promised to enter the land because they believed in the greatness and promises of God!

After Moses had passed away, Joshua became the new leader of Israel and would lead them into the promised land. Caleb and Joshua had to wait over forty years to get their promise. One of my favorite parts of this story is what Caleb asked Joshua:

> *"And now, behold, the Lord has kept me alive, as He said, these forty-five years, ever since the Lord spoke this word to Moses while Israel wandered in the wilderness; and now, here I am this day, eighty-five years old. As yet I am as strong this day as on the day that Moses sent me; just as my strength was then, so now is my strength for war, both for going out and for coming in. Now therefore, **give me this mountain** of which the Lord spoke in that day; for you heard in that day how the Anakim were there, and that the cities were great and fortified. It may be that the Lord will be with*

> *me, and I shall be able to drive them out as the Lord said."* (emphasis added)
>
> Joshua 14:10–12

Whoa! Caleb at eighty-five years old asked for the mountain that the "giants" lived on. That is bold faith! God had not only kept him alive, but he had apparently not even aged (that is really a good deal). He went on to conquer that mountain that he asked for; nothing is too hard when the Lord is with us!

Understanding Opposites

This may sound pretty basic, but the devil and God are opposites. God is love and the devil is hate. The devil wants you to live in fear, poverty, and disease, but God wants you to be courageous (like Caleb and Joshua), to be prosperous, and be completely whole in every area of your body. The Bible says in Jeremiah 29:11 that God has a good plan for your life, and we can be sure that the devil has a bad one—one to kill, steal, and destroy (John 10:10). God wants to give you life and life more abundantly. That sounds like "greatness," doesn't it? God loves each one of us unconditionally and calls us His sons and daughters. The devil just *uses* people for his benefit, and they get no rewards for it in hell. God will actually reward us for what we do for Him (Revelation 22:12)! Our heavenly Father is so good!

Therefore, understand that our heavenly Father delights in making us the head and not the tail, prospering the righteous (Psalm 112:3), and giving us the desires of our heart (Psalm 37:4).

Four Big Dis-es and their Opposites

The latin prefix "dis" generally means "not" or "opposite of."[2] Therefore, I'm going to list some "dis-es" that the devil uses against us and show the opposite side of victory with God when we remove the "dis":

— *Discourage:* The devil loves to try to take away our courage by getting us to focus on the giants (the problems) in our lives. If we remove the "dis," then we get *"courage."* The phrase "fear not" appears numerous times in the Bible. Therefore, every day we should choose to embrace God's courage. The Bible says God didn't give us a spirit of fear (2 Timothy 1:7).

— *Disappoint:* The devil loves to remind us of how many times people have disappointed us or even how we have disappointed ourselves by not meeting goals and desires we were reaching for. However, if you take away the "dis", you get the word "appoint." I remember one day several years ago when I was praying in my backyard about some disappointments I had faced, and I heard the Lord tell me, *"The devil wants to disappoint you, but I want to appoint you!"* Zephaniah 3:19 says, *"...I will appoint them for praise and fame in every land where they were put to shame."* This scripture is what God wants to do for His saints in this nation and around the world. We have been *"shamed"* for our biblical beliefs, but God is about to appoint us for fame!

— *Disable:* The devil likes to try to make us feel unable to fulfill our destiny with a feeling of weakness or to just overwhelm us with focusing on our inadequacies. If you take away the "dis," you get the word *"able"*. Caleb said to the people in Numbers 13:30, *"…Let us go up at once and take possession, for we are well **able** to overcome it."* (emphasis added)

— *Disqualify*: The devil likes to make us feel unworthy to do the things God has put on our heart. He likes to remind us of past mistakes and failures in order to make us *feel* disqualified and inadequate to move forward in our gifts and callings. However, Jesus has qualified us at the cross. We read in Colossians 1:12, *"giving thanks to the Father who has **qualified** us to be partakers of the inheritance of the saints in the light."* (emphasis added) Therefore, we need to remove the "dis" and know that Jesus has made us qualified!

Therefore, we need to be mindful about choosing and fighting for the positive mindsets God has for us and rejecting the negative mindsets the devil wants us to have. Not only do we need to conquer mountains in our nation, but we also all have personal mountains to conquer. We each have dreams and Godly desires that God has put within us. Believe God for your mountains! Kick the "dis-es" and the "giants" out of your life and your family's lives. Boldly go after your promised land!

In summary, whatever the devil is doing, God is doing the opposite. I know this is simple, but it is something we have to be reminded about sometimes. When the devil is trying to take down our country's economy and liberty, then God has plans to prosper us and "Make America Great Again." The devil will lose, because our God is the winner and *always* has the final say.

Therefore, believe God for big things! It's time to take the land!

> *Do not fear, little flock, for it is your Father's good pleasure to give you the kingdom.*
> Luke 12:32

TRUE LIBERTY

Chapter 11

> *Now the Lord is the Spirit; and where the Spirit of the Lord is, there is liberty.*
>
> 2 Corinthians 3:17

One of the key lines in our Declaration of Independence is as follows:

> "We hold these truths to be self-evident, that all men are created equal, that they are endowed by their Creator with certain unalienable Rights, that among these are Life, Liberty and the pursuit of Happiness."

I love that our founding fathers recognized that our Creator, God, is the one who gives us equality, life, liberty, and the pursuit of happiness. This again reminds me of this scripture:

> *The thief does not come except to steal, and to kill, and to destroy. I have come that they may have life, and that they may have it more abundantly.*
>
> John 10:10

To put it bluntly, God wants us to have a great life and the devil wants us to have a miserable one. The good life we all desire only comes from God! Anyone who takes away your God-given liberty is not your friend. The liberal agenda has wanted to decide *for us* whether or not we feel comfortable with a new, unproven vaccine. They want to tell us whether we can have church or not. The social media police want to tell us what we can and cannot say. This is not the liberty God gave us. Just like how those who went before us fought wars to ensure that we keep our liberty values here in America, we now face a cultural war to keep our freedoms.

Bondage versus Liberty

I love the book of Galatians! To me, the whole book of Galatians in the Bible is one of liberty and exhorting us to keep our liberty that Jesus died for us to have. Obviously, the opposite of liberty is bondage, and the Apostle Paul was careful to explain to the Church of Galatia what the difference is between the two. I believe that Galatians is the New Testament counterpart to Deuteronomy 28 in the Old

Testament. Let me explain: in the entire chapter of Deuteronomy 28, God speaks to Israel in detail the blessings for them if they obey the Lord and the consequences (curses) if they disobey. It is noteworthy to notice that the list of the curses were explained in much longer detail than the list of the blessings. I believe God wanted to be sure that He explained the curses in enough detail to cause them to not want to go that route. In fact, just in case they still didn't understand, God gave them the right answer in Deuteronomy 30:19, "*I call heaven and earth as witnesses today against you, that I have set before you life and death, blessing and cursing; therefore **choose life**, that both you and your descendants may live*" (emphasis added). In Galatians, Paul teaches the Christians to choose the new covenant of grace, and to not go back to the old covenant of law.

Paul addressed in Galatians that going back to the Old Covenant laws after Jesus established the New Covenant of Grace is putting yourself under bondage. In fact, Paul stood up to the Apostle Peter for his hypocrisy of not eating with the uncircumcised Gentiles when he was with the circumcised Jews. (All people were equal under this better new covenant when they are born-again.) Circumcision was a requirement God gave under the Old Covenant, but under the New Covenant, it is a circumcision of the heart (Romans 2:29). In the following scriptures, Paul calls the Galatians foolish for allowing such bondage:

> *O foolish Galatians! Who has bewitched you that you should not obey the truth, before whose eyes Jesus Christ was clearly portrayed among you as crucified? This only I want to learn from you: Did you receive the Spirit by the works of the law, or by the hearing of faith? Are you so foolish? Having begun in the Spirit, are you now being made*

> *perfect by the flesh? Have you suffered so many things in vain—if indeed it was in vain?*
> Galatians 3:1–4

Therefore, for the Galatians to go back to an inferior covenant when Jesus had paid the price for this amazing new covenant was foolish. For us in America, this would be politically the equivalent of allowing corrupt politicians to put us under a dictatorship type of control by taking away many of our personal liberties when so many previous Americans fought and died to give us those liberties. Millions of people have left those types of countries to come to ours so they can be free. Our United States Constitution and Declaration of Independence are a much superior political system to that of being under a dictator-type ruler, like the king of England, George III, who we were in bondage to before we became our own nation.

Another bondage spoken of in Galatians is the works of the flesh (sin), as described in Galatians 5:19–21. Then, Paul describes the blessings of having the fruit of the Holy Spirit, as described in Galatians 5:22–23. Here is another example of being under the curse versus being under God's blessings. We have been experiencing in America and other parts of the world resistance towards biblical values. There are many that feel biblical values are outdated and take away personal liberties, but we as Christians know that is not true. True Christianity *gives* liberty because there is no liberty apart from God (2 Corinthians 3:17). We also know that sin produces bondage. For example, a person addicted to illegal drugs is in bondage to those drugs. A person who is addicted to any kind of sin is in bondage to that sin:

> *Do you not know that to whom you present yourselves slaves to obey, you are that one's*

> *slaves whom you obey, whether of sin leading to death, or of obedience leading to righteousness?*
> Romans 6:16

Living like God wants us to live is freedom and life. Therefore, for a society to be free, there must be biblical values in every area of our culture.

I thought it was very significant what Paul said concerning how the wrong doctrines were being introduced to the Galatians:

> *And this occurred because of false brethren secretly brought in (who came in by stealth to spy out our liberty which we have in Christ Jesus, that they might bring us into bondage)*
> Galatians 2:4

In other words, Paul is addressing that wolves dressed in sheep's clothing pretending to be Christian leaders had come to purposely take away their New Covenant liberty in Jesus! I felt immediately that the Lord highlighted how this can easily apply to our liberty in America. There are some people right now sitting in political offices that pretend to be for American values; however, when they speak, the policies they are for are clearly anti-American with socialistic/communistic values. I believe there are many people with anti-American ideologies that have purposely been planted in key governmental positions, and we must pray for God to remove those with wrong motives.

> *Beware of false prophets, who come to you in sheep's clothing, but inwardly they are ravenous wolves. You will know them by their*

> *fruits. Do men gather grapes from thornbushes or figs from thistles?*
>
> Matthew 7:15–16

We have been in a season in America when the enemy has come to spy out our freedom (Galatians 2:4) and take us into bondage, and we need to daily ask God for truth. When I say "enemy," I don't necessarily mean people, because we are in a spiritual battle; however, the enemy (the devil) uses people with wrong motives to take us into bondage. Policies that take away the American citizens' basic rights like religious freedoms, freedom of speech, freedom to educate our children with Godly values, along with other important Godly values, lead to bondage.

In Galatians 2:4, when Paul addressed the fact that *"false brethren"* had come among them, I believe this is also a type of the parable of the wheat and tares (Matthew 13:24–30). Just like false brethren can look like true brethren, tares in a wheat field can look very similar to the wheat. Jesus said in Matthew 7:16 that we will know the difference by their fruit. For example, in politics, when a politician does the opposite of what they told you they would do when they campaigned for your votes, take notice of that. One of the things many of us love about Donald Trump is that he did what he promised he would do. He is honest, and that is a quality we want leaders to have!

A couple of other examples of the fake and the real would be the following: in Christianity, you can sit in a church and not really have committed yourself to Jesus. Therefore, sitting in a church does not make you a Christian. Making Jesus your Savior *does* make you a Christian. This principle can also apply to American citizens. For example, you can be an American citizen by law and even hold political offices, but if you have not embraced America's core values of liberty and justice for all, then perhaps you are not an American patriot at heart. Thus also, you can live in another country but believe in American values and thus be more American than someone born here that actually hates our country and its core values. Paul addressed this concept in Romans concerning Israel:

> *…For they are not all Israel who are of Israel*
> Romans 9:6

Paul was addressing the fact that just because someone was a resident of Israel does not mean they were in keeping with the values of God's covenant with Israel. When it comes to the spiritual fight we have been in over keeping America's Christian values of liberty and constitutional values, there are some Americans that are not for America, and there are people from other countries that are for us. For example, people who hold our American values in other countries have more in common with us than someone here who is burning flags and teaching communism.

I'll give you a personal example: a couple of years ago I made some dear friends from South Korea through the *School of Revival* online Christian group that I described in chapter five. They even came and visited my family and I in the summer of 2021. I told my friends, Hacksun and Seya Cha, about this book I have been working on, and they have been praying for me ever since. Also, I found out that they have been praying for America for many years; they had noticed how the enemy was trying to take away our liberty. I still remember how touching it was to hear them tell our group how they, along with many other South Koreans, were so thankful for the Americans that fought for their freedom in South Korea in the past. Therefore, I consider my friends *Americans in spirit* because they love America and the values we hold dear. I have noticed that so many Christians around the world have been praying for us, and we appreciate it so much!

Until time is no more and Jesus has returned to rule and reign, we will have to carefully guard our freedoms. The devil is just way too happy to bring us into bondage in any way he can, so we have to be discerning of his tactics. In Galatians 5:1 we read, *"Stand fast therefore in the liberty by which Christ has made us free, and do not be entangled again with a yoke of bondage."* Notice it says "not to be entangled *again."* How many of us know that it is human nature to repeat history, when it is a lot smarter to learn from history. Whether it be our own bad choices in the past or national bad choices, we should have learned something from the past. We know from world history that whenever a country departs from Christian values and embraces some sort of dictatorship, that country normally ends up in terrible bondage and poverty for most of the people (except the ruling class of course).

Stand Firm in our Liberty

In the New International Version of the Bible, Galatians 5:1 reads like this:

> *It is for freedom that Christ has set us free.* **Stand firm**, *then, and do not let yourselves be burdened again by a yoke of slavery.* (emphasis added)
> Galatians 5:1 (NIV)

The greek word for "stand firm" in the above verse is "stekete" which means: *to stand, stand firm*[1] . Since the NKJV uses the words "stand fast," I want to point out the definition of "standfast" when you put the two words together. "Standfast" is *a rigid or unyielding position.*[2] I know for myself, being compliant is sometimes easier than holding my ground about an issue. We as Christians generally are peace-loving people. We want to love people, not have to make uncomfortable and unpopular stands. My friend, Gabby, however, enjoys making stands better than I do, so I have learned much from our friendship. For example, Gabby made stands in very liberal places that she was not going to violate her freedom to breathe fresh air by wearing the mask and probably was the only person in certain stores not wearing it. I really admire her courage! (At the time, she was living on the west coast.) I live on the opposite side of the country (east coast) in a more conservative state, and therefore, it was not as strict here; most of the time I didn't wear the mask, but to be honest, that didn't take much courage where I live! I mainly didn't like my glasses to fog up or feel like I was suffocating! However, the truth is that it's been proven the masks don't work, and most of us have figured out by now that it was merely obedience training from those who desire to control us.

In order for us to "stand firm" in our freedoms, we (including myself) need to make bold stands for truth more and more and not surrender to falsehoods. The Bible says that *truth* is freedom:

> *And you shall know the truth, and the truth shall make you free.*
>
> John 8:32

The opposite of truth is "lies," and many understand that lies will put you in some kind of bondage. If a used car salesman tells you the car you want is in excellent condition, but you find out six months down the road that you have a lemon, then that lie has put you in a financial bondage with repairs. In worst case scenarios, lies can kill you. If you were to befriend someone who is actually a murderer, but they have painted themselves as a saint, then the lies the person is telling you to get you to believe they are a great person has put your life in danger.

This is why it has been a dangerous and evil thing for the fake news media to purposely propagate lies to deceive the American people. Their agenda was to take away our liberty by getting people to believe a lie and therefore cause their listeners to trust people (like Joe Biden) who were not trustworthy and not trust people (like Donald Trump) who were actually trustworthy. It reminds me of the scripture I quoted in a previous chapter (Isaiah 5:20) in which Isaiah laments how some call evil good and good evil.

It is important that we always ask God to reveal truth to us and to allow us to notice when we are being lied to. We should always be quick to tell the truth and not allow people to intimidate us into silence. The Bible tells us in Romans 1:16 to not be ashamed of the gospel. We must also not be silent when we see injustices, corruption, and lies in our society. Therefore, to keep our republic, we must be bold in standing for truth. We must "**stand firm**" in what we know to be God's truth!

True liberty was purchased at the cross for us by Jesus Christ. There is no liberty apart from Him. Therefore, if we want liberty in our nation, we need to honor Jesus in our nation. Jesus is the one who made the United States of America famous for liberty, because our founding fathers dedicated this nation to Him!

Our nation's current official Pledge of Allegiance states:

> *"I pledge allegiance to the flag of the United States of America, and to the republic for which it stands, one nation under God, indivisible, with liberty and justice for all."*

I love the words, *"one nation under God."* When we are under God, we are under His blessings and His protection. We should never assume that our nation came to be great without being under God's favor and protection. As I said in a previous chapter, we are in the valley of decision, and we need to choose greatness, choose life, and choose liberty, which equals having God in our decisions and allowing him to bless us and protect us.

Having Christian liberty does not mean we exile people belonging to other religions, but it does mean we are loving, kind, and respectful to all people, being a Christian example of a nation following Jesus. God, the Father, treats all humans with the same respect. He hopes that all will accept Jesus as Savior and spend eternity in heaven; however, if you choose not to, He will not force salvation on you, nor will He remove you from the planet! He will give you every chance possible to choose Him.

We are in a season where God's people have been crying out for liberty around this world, and I believe we will get liberty soon. There have been very many prophetic promises from reliable voices that the Lion of Judah is on his way for a showdown. Liberty is God's Spirit being poured out on us. We can only go so far with man-made laws, even though it is important to make them prayerfully in alignment with God. However, true liberty reigns in our heart when we have made Jesus Lord of our lives. The Bible says that God will write His laws in our hearts (Hebrews 8:10). We must allow God to fill us with His Holy Spirit to have His kind of liberty:

> *I will put My Spirit within you and cause you to walk in My statutes, and you will keep My judgments and do them.*
>
> Ezekiel 36:27

> *But the fruit of the Spirit is love, joy, peace, longsuffering, kindness, goodness, faithfulness, gentleness, self-control.* **Against such there is no law.** (emphasis added)
>
> Galatians 5:22–23

I love how in Galatians 5:23, Paul says that when we walk in the fruit of the Spirit, basically there is no need for the law. However, the law is for the lawless, and we will need laws until Jesus returns. But for those of us who follow God, we should be treating people with love and kindness like the Lord treats us.

My Personal Testimony of Needing to Stand Firm for my Liberty in an Area of my Life

I gave some of my Christian testimony in a previous chapter concerning the church where I was born again in the early 80s. Because of the overemphasis on spiritual authority and submission to leaders, my very sensitive nature and willingness to please God was put in a lot of bondage. I had lots of fear and even panic attacks. When I came out of that church and the Lord began to teach me what real freedom in Him was—how He had paid the ultimate price for my freedom and my gift of righteousness—it was a journey to embrace this freedom.

I remember one time being at another church that is still to this day one of my favorites, if I were only to consider my first few years of attending. The preaching was full of faith and the worship carried such a weighty anointing and presence of God. However, after some time, I began to notice some changes in behavior that didn't feel right in my spirit. My friend, Judy, who also attended the same church, was also having concerns, so we began having weekly prayer times together for the church. I still remember one Sunday when I called my friend to tell her a disturbing dream I had, and then found out she had the same dream! We both dreamed the night before that we had divorced our husbands and were about to marry a worldly guy who was smoking cigarettes! Just to let you know, Judy and I are not perfect people, but we are *definitely* not the type to do something like that! We both love our husbands and love Jesus! (We are also both allergic to cigarette smoke!) Well, God was able to use that dream to give us spiritual understanding that the leadership of this church was taking a turn away from God back into the world, which gave us the direction we needed in prayer.

Eventually, after not seeing any changes from our prayer times, the Lord led my husband and I, and my friend, Judy, to leave this church and attend somewhere else even though we kept praying for this pastor. My friend Judy had taught me that sometimes it is safer to pray from a distance! However, it really bothered me for some time after leaving this church because it is in my nature to be loyal, and I questioned myself many times if we did the right thing. There really wasn't anything serious that we knew of factually taking place, only small things, but we were sensing something dark in our prayer times. Therefore, we didn't really have any solid foundation to validate leaving. There were many times that I desired to go back and at least visit, but I would open my Bible in prayer and it would fall on *Galatians 5:1* so often: "Stand fast in the liberty in which Christ has made you free…" Seriously, it would happen so often that I began to get the point that God was saying, "no—do not go back!" Then, one day, I realized that this church had begun live streaming and thought there would be no harm in tuning in online one time from home. (Yes, I had not fully gotten God's point yet!)

I was shocked when I found the senior pastor's message to be leaving the basic fundamentals of Christianity. For example, the pastor no longer believed there was an actual hell, and he said that everybody went to heaven. (We know all dogs *and cats* go to heaven, but people have to make a choice for Jesus!) This teaching violated what we know to be the truth that you only get to heaven by making Jesus your Savior. He is the door and there is no other! Later, there were more serious scandals that became public, and they lost their church.

Therefore, it is important that we are led by the Spirit. It is true that most of the time we need to show grace and overlook people's faults; however, there are times when staying somewhere or putting up with something could lead you into bondage and deception. We need to avoid the entrapment and stand firm in our liberty in Jesus. The Apostle Paul said in 1 Corinthians 5:6, *"…Do you know that a little leaven leavens the whole lump?"* In the gospel, Jesus taught that leaven could represent the false doctrines of the Pharisees and Herod (Mark 8:15). For us today, that would represent false teaching in the Church and also corruption and lies from government leaders.

—— Not Putting up with Bondage ——

In 1 Corinthians 11, Paul admonishes the Corinthians for listening to false teachers that were bringing them into bondage. He did not mince words and even got a little sarcastic; he was upset like a good parent is when your kids listen to the wrong voices!

> *But I fear, lest somehow, as the serpent deceived Eve by his craftiness, so your minds*

> *may be corrupted from the simplicity that is in Christ. For if he who comes preaches another Jesus whom we have not preached, or if you receive a different spirit which you have not received, or a different gospel which you have not accepted—you may well put up with it!*
>
> 2 Corinthians 11:3–4

Notice that the above verse says that the devil wants to take you away from the *"simplicity that is in Christ."* In those beginning Christian years when my personal mentor and friend was teaching me the difference in having a relationship with God versus religious bondages full of man-made rules that didn't come from God, one of the key principles she taught me was this in simple form: the devil is complicated and God is simple. For example, if you have ever had to go for some kind of spiritual deliverance, you would find that the spirits of darkness that had polluted your life usually look like a tangled spider web. It is all connected together. If you have a spirit of fear, you may have gotten it because you were abandoned mentally or physically at some time in your life, also connecting it to a spirit of abandonment. The abandonment can be connected to a spirit of rejection, and so forth. God is simple in the fact that when you receive Him into your life, you receive everything heaven has potentially. In one name (Jesus), all demons have to flee. Also, there is one way to heaven: Jesus. It's that simple!

The political equivalent of this principle of simplicity versus complication is when there is an excess of government laws. The 700 Club did a wonderful series several years ago called "*A Nation of Criminals*"[3] where they highlighted stories of average Americans that had gotten in severe legal trouble, usually over a law most people didn't know existed. We found out from this program that there were thousands of laws that the average person doesn't know about. Some of these stories had to do with environmental laws broken, for example. Most of the people interviewed did not know they had done anything wrong initially, and the punishment meted out seemed extreme. My personal take away from that series is that we must simplify things when it comes to federal regulations; don't make more laws than the average person even knows exists. That can be a big setup to make it easy to take someone down you don't like!

Paul loved the people he taught enough to warn them about the dangers of losing their God-given liberty. You see, the tactics of the devil to bring you into any kind of bondage and/or deception is not usually so noticeable at first. He does not come to your door in full costume, with the red suit and pitchfork, because you would probably slam your door and lock it. No, the Bible says he comes as an angel of light (2 Corinthians 11:14). An angel of light means he is trying to look good—he is wearing an angel costume, but he is still the devil and ugly underneath. The devil usually does things progressively, a little bit at a time, to make it less obvious what is happening, which is why we need to ask God for discernment.

Big government and corrupt leaders many times appear to give you promises of a better life, but this is what the Apostle Peter had to say about that:

> *While they promise them liberty, they themselves are slaves of corruption; for by whom a person is overcome, by him also he is brought into bondage.*
>
> 2 Peter 2:19

The devil has a million and one ways to trap you into sin or bondage, but God has one way to get you out of it—offering salvation through receiving Jesus Christ as your personal Savior. Jesus is our answer to any problem we have. We can come boldly before His throne of grace for help (Hebrews 4:16).

We need to not put up with bondage. We have the choice to "say no":

> *For you put up with fools gladly, since you yourselves are wise! For you put up with it if one brings you into bondage, if one devours you, if one takes from you, if one exalts himself, if one strikes you on the face.*
>
> 2 Corinthians 11:19–20

I know in my own personal walk with the Lord, my personality naturally wants to walk in love and be very forgiving towards people, which of course, we always should do: love and forgive. However, the Lord had to teach me the hard way that love and forgiveness does not equal being a "doormat." You can love and forgive from a distance. We should not put up with any kind of abuse or bondage.

Socialism and communism will devour you and put you into bondage. Not being able to make your own health decisions will put you into bondage. Not being able to educate your children with truth and Christian values will put you into bondage. Listening to fake news will put you into bondage. Corrupt politicians who want to deceive you and control you will put you into bondage. Say "no" to bondage at the ballot boxes, say "no" by contacting politicians with your opinions. We must use our voices to "say no." We must learn to *not put up with* bondage, whether in our nation or in our personal lives. Jesus died to give us liberty!

—— What Does Liberty Look Like in a Nation?

What does a nation of liberty look like? It will look beautiful—that is how it will look! Since liberty comes from our Creator and the Bible teaches us that where God's Spirit is, there is liberty (2 Corinthians 3:17), then liberty looks like our God!

Liberty looks like God's blessings, not the curse:

> *The blessing of the Lord makes one rich,*
> *And He adds no sorrow with it.*
> Proverbs 10:22

God wants to prosper a nation that honors Him. God's blessing wants to make us healthy, wealthy, and wise!

> *Blessed be the God and Father of our Lord Jesus Christ, who has blessed us with every spiritual blessing in the heavenly places in Christ*
> Ephesians 1:3

When I think of a nation of liberty, I think of having leaders that you know want what is best for the people they serve. Think of it personally: do you want to be in a relationship that only *pretends* to care for you, but is secretly trying to destroy you? Of course not, we want relationships which we can trust and know to have our back. Politically, we have seen corruption on a level that leads to many not knowing who to trust. We need to pray and believe that God is going to do such a reformation on every level of government that we have people serving that really *care* about the well-being of Americans. Jesus taught us the characteristics of a good leader:

> *I am the good shepherd. The good shepherd gives His life for the sheep. But a hireling, he who is not the shepherd, one who does not own the sheep, sees the wolf coming and leaves the sheep and flees; and the wolf catches the sheep and scatters them. The hireling flees because he is a hireling and does not care about the sheep.*
>
> John 10:11–13

Translating the above scripture in political language, good shepherds are politicians who serve, care, and protect the citizens of America. The hirelings are swamp creatures who are in it for their own gain and don't care what the negative consequences of their decisions are for the American people as long as it gets them what they want! Translating this in Church language is the same: true leaders are to serve and care for God's people, not take advantage of them or put them into some kind of bondage. I like to say that if you leave a church service feeling worse than you came, and it takes you three hours in prayer to feel better, then maybe you need to look for another place! Here is a scripture that has meant a lot to me:

> *The remnant of Israel shall do no unrighteousness and speak no lies, nor shall a deceitful tongue be found in their mouth; for they shall feed their flocks and lie down, and no one shall make them afraid.*
>
> Zephaniah 3:13

God wants to give us leaders in all areas of society who we can trust and who will make us feel safe. This will put us in a place and season of rest. Fear comes when we are surrounded by people who are untrustworthy, which causes us to not be at rest. Psalm 23 is a great example of how God wants to lead us and take care of us!

God has a good plan for America. The Bible says to taste and see that the Lord is good (Psalm 34:8). His kind of freedom is good. He wants us to be blessed in every area of our lives. Freedom isn't free. Jesus paid a high price to give us the luxury of freedom. Also, many soldiers have died in American wars to gain our freedom and keep our freedoms. The best way to honor their sacrifices is to *stay free*. I believe they are cheering us on from the cloud of witnesses.

I'm reminded of the song written by Lee Greenwood, "God Bless the USA," released in 1984. Here is a portion of the lyrics:

> And I'm proud to be an American
> Where at least I know I'm free
> And I won't forget the men who died
> Who gave that right to me
> And I'd gladly stand up next to you
> And defend Her still today
> 'Cause there ain't no doubt
> I love this land
> God Bless the U.S.A.

A Season of Jubilee

I believe we are about to enter a season of "Jubilee."

> *'And you shall count seven sabbaths of years for yourself, seven times seven years; and the time of the seven sabbaths of years shall be to you forty-nine years. Then you shall cause the trumpet of the Jubilee to sound on the tenth day of the seventh month; on the Day of Atonement you shall make the trumpet to sound throughout all your land. And you shall consecrate the fiftieth year, and proclaim liberty throughout all the land to all its inhabitants. It shall be a Jubilee for you; and each of you shall return to his possession, and each of you shall return to his family. That fiftieth year shall be a Jubilee to you; in it you shall neither sow nor reap what grows of its own accord, nor gather the grapes of your untended vine. For it is the Jubilee; it shall be holy to you; you shall eat its produce from the field.*
>
> *In this Year of Jubilee, each of you shall return to his possession.'*
>
> Leviticus 25:8–13

God had made a law in Israel for every fiftieth year to be a year of Jubilee. This was a special time of liberty for the Jewish nation in which people could receive properties back, slaves were set free, and they and the land had a year of rest. Jesus is our Jubilee now, and we can always have Jubilee with Jesus!

> *The Spirit of the Lord is upon Me, because He has anointed Me to preach the gospel to the poor; He has sent Me to heal the brokenhearted, to proclaim liberty to the captives and recovery of sight to the blind, to set at liberty those who are oppressed; to proclaim the acceptable year of the Lord.*
>
> Luke 4:18–19

However, in our political times and seasons in America and around the world, we have been in a season of God rooting out corruption that has taken our freedoms. I found it prophetic that in the passages in Leviticus 25, the "trumpet" announced the year of Jubilee. I believe Donald Trump has been a trumpet—a voice to point out the corruption that many of us didn't see and bring great governmental reformation. God's prophets have also been trumpets to reveal what God has been saying in this season.

Personally, I love the meaning that we can get out of the customs of the year of Jubilee in the Bible. It reminds me of how we all need a "do over" sometimes. We get ourselves in a mess, and we need God to get us out of it. Our land needs to rest, and our bodies need a rest from the battles of life. Jubilee was a time of freedom from bondages and was also a rest for the land. Jubilee was also a great time of celebration for the Jews, and spiritually, we are about to enter a season of celebration from the war we have been in. Let's not forget to enjoy it!

Patrick Henry, one of our founding fathers, gave a famous speech on March 23, 1775, in which he spoke these famous words at the end: "*I know not what course others may take; but as for me, give me liberty or give me death!*" Our country was founded on the basis of liberty, one that would carry God's kind of liberty. **We choose liberty**!

THE REBIRTH OF AMERICA

Chapter 12

> *Who has heard such a thing?*
> *Who has seen such things?*
> *Shall the earth be made to give birth in one day?*
> *Or shall a nation be born at once?*
> *For as soon as Zion was in labor,*
> *She gave birth to her children.*
>
> Isaiah 66:8

CAN A NATION BE BORN IN A DAY?

The answer is *yes*, of course, when it is God, because *all things are possible with God* (Matthew 19:26). I believe we are about to see amazing changes take place, where one day things are one way, and they are completely flipped the next day.

> "Look among the nations and watch—
> Be utterly astounded!
> For I will work a work in your days
> Which you would not believe,
>   though it were told you."
>
> Habakkuk 1:5

The Lord has used the above scripture many times to encourage me over our nation and world. We are in a season of surprises from our Father God. He has heard the cries of His people all over the world, and we are about to see major changes in all areas of society. It is going to be so much better than we imagined, just like the scripture in Ephesians 3:20, *"Now to Him who is able to do exceedingly abundantly above all that we ask or think, according to the power that works in us."*

Usually when something happens quickly, the whole process has not been quick. There usually has been underground work for some time, but the manifestation can be quick. For example, women are pregnant with a baby for nine months, but the time of delivery usually happens within a day. The pregnancy was much longer however!

In the United States of America, there have been many years of prayer for God to make positive changes and deliver us from corruption. God has been working on our behalf behind the scenes all along. Angels on assignment have been fighting spiritual forces. Some of the progress we have seen, as corruption has been publicly exposed, but some things we won't know about until later. However, there have been a few prophetic voices that have said that the actual breakthrough (miraculous deliverance) will really take place in a twenty-four hour period. So hang in there saints, the breakthrough is coming!

Can a Nation be Born Again?

In John 3:1–21, we read how Jesus explained to Nicodemus, a Pharisee, that he must be born again:

> *Jesus answered and said to him, "Most assuredly, I say to you, unless one is born again, he cannot see the kingdom of God."*
> John 3:3

When we ask Jesus to be Lord of our lives, we become born again. Because this is a spiritual rebirth, not a natural rebirth, we may look the same on the outside, but our hearts and minds have been transformed. We are now a new creation in Christ (2 Corinthians 5:17)—old things have passed away and all things have become new!

What I believe God is going to do as He pours out His Spirit on our nation is do a transformation where God will be honored in this nation in a way that most of us have not seen in our lifetimes. We will still be the United States of America, but this land will be filled with God's presence and glory. This will bring positive transformation to all parts of society. I believe America as a nation will have a born again experience!

The Red Sea Deliverance

In Exodus 1–14, we read how Israel, who had been in a long period (400 years) of slavery in Egypt, got miraculously delivered from bondage. God had raised up Moses, an Israelite by birth that was raised by Pharaoh's daughter, to stand up to Pharaoh and lead them out of bondage. However, the process was messy, and sometimes, things looked like they were going in the opposite direction, before their deliverance came to fruition.

For example, after Moses heard from God in the wilderness, and he came back to Egypt to tell his Israelite brethren that God had answered their cries for deliverance, it took ten plagues before they were free to go. Moses and his brother, Aaron, repeatedly went to Pharaoh saying *"Let My People Go,"* but Pharaoh repeatedly hardened his heart, resulting in God sending plagues to Egypt. The Israelites still were slaves doing hard manual labor for the Egyptians, which was bad enough; however, now on top of a hard job, they lost their favor with the Egyptian leaders during the plagues, and Pharoah made things even tougher on them!

> *So the same day Pharaoh commanded the taskmasters of the people and their officers, saying, "You shall no longer give the people straw to make brick as before. Let them go and gather straw for themselves. And you shall lay on them the quota of bricks which they made before. You shall not reduce it. For they are idle; therefore they cry out, saying, 'Let us go and sacrifice to our God.' Let more work be laid on the men, that they may labor in it, and let them not regard false words."*
>
> Exodus 5:6–9

What happened to Israel is not uncommon to any of us. One of the tactics of the devil when God has given us personally a big promise of breakthrough or even prophetic promises as a nation is to try to discourage us and get us off of our faith walk by making things look worse. The devil is hoping we will give up.

For example, there were many prophetic voices that said Donald Trump would win a second term in the 2020 election; some later thought the prophets got it wrong because of Biden taking office. However, there has been more than enough evidence of fraud and the truth is—he did win, and he won by a landslide! I remember how I personally thought that God would have saved the day BEFORE Biden was inaugurated on January 20, 2021. However, when that didn't happen, God spoke very clearly to me that there would be a Red Sea experience where we would receive a great deliverance from the corruption and fraud we had experienced. Of course, I thought *that* would happen in the next few months after God told me!

Have you ever noticed that when God gives an amazing promise, we *assume* He is about to do it right away? I'm sure the Jews thought that when Jesus said He was coming back soon; they would have never thought that God's soon is not the same as our soon! We want the drive-through window kind of soon. We don't want to suffer while we are waiting. However, the Bible says that our trials are producing patience:

> *My brethren, count it all joy when you fall into various trials, knowing that the testing of your faith produces patience. But let patience have its perfect work, that you may be perfect and complete, lacking nothing.*
>
> James 1:2–4

Therefore, as I'm completing this book in the summer of 2023, I feel like we are toward the end of our trial and the Red Sea breakthrough is soon. Israel did not expect their breakthrough to take so long and when it finally happened, things had gotten worse for them before getting better. In Exodus 14, they ended up trapped between Pharaoh's army and the Red Sea, which was definitely what we call between a rock and a hard place, yet their biggest breakthrough was about to happen. In fact, as they cried out to Moses in fear, they lost all hope and faith in that moment:

> *And when Pharaoh drew near, the children of Israel lifted their eyes, and behold, the Egyptians marched after them. So they were very afraid, and the children of Israel cried out to the Lord. Then they said to Moses, "Because there were no graves in Egypt, have you taken us away to die in the wilderness? Why have you so dealt with us, to bring us up out of Egypt? Is this not the word that we told you in Egypt, saying, 'Let us alone that we may serve the Egyptians'? For it would have been better for us to serve the Egyptians than that we should die in the wilderness."*
>
> Exodus 14:10–12

Poor Moses! They could certainly be a whiny bunch of people at times, but if we are honest, we all have our whiny times when our flesh speaks instead of our spirit man of faith. Yet, what did God tell Moses?

> *And the Lord said to Moses, "Why do you cry to Me? Tell the children of Israel to go forward. But lift up your rod, and stretch out your hand over the sea and divide it. And the children of Israel shall go on dry ground through the midst of the sea."*
>
> Exodus 14:15–16

How many times does God say something similar to us? When we feel like we are stuck in the worst possible situation, God says to use your rod of authority, speak to the circumstances, and go forward!

And yes, God did even more than they expected. I love how in Ephesians 3:20, we are promised that God will do exceedingly, abundantly, more than we can ask or think. Not only did God split the Red Sea and let them walk to the other side on dry ground, but with the same ocean that God used to take them to the other side, He destroyed all of Pharaoh's army as they chased them through the Red Sea. We don't know what the Egyptians were thinking when they ran through that Red Sea, but they were not very smart! One reason people who are on the dark side do dumb things is because of their pride. Since they are following the devil and he is full of pride, they get the same spirit of pride and they self-destruct. I love this verse, which has been a personal one God uses for me when I need encouragement:

> *Then the waters returned and covered the chariots, the horsemen, and all the army of Pharaoh that came into the sea after them. **Not so much as one of them remained**.*" (emphasis added)
> Exodus 14:28

Wow, at the same time God was delivering Israel, He was destroying ALL of their enemies! I have heard many ministers say that many times it becomes the darkest right before the breakthrough! Of course, in today's times, I'm speaking of our spiritual enemies being destroyed (Ephesians 6:12), not our natural enemies physically dying. We desire that people in leadership positions that have evil agendas lose their positions and influence, but we should always forgive them and pray for their salvation.

I love how God always turns things to the good when people have to go through difficult battles. Like for instance, when Israel got delivered from the worst job ever, *slavery*, they headed toward the promised land with the wealth given to them before they left. And to top it off, God destroyed their enemies so they would not have to be nervous in the wilderness, looking over their shoulder constantly. That is the icing on the cake, my friends. God is good, and we are going to see His goodness poured out on His Church around the world and also our nation along with others. What has seemed to be like our worst season is actually going to lead us to our best season!

Our Best Days Are Yet to Come

God is about to do a divine flip in our country and bring us into days of prosperity and greatness. This will be a new wineskin for America. We need to clean out the survival thinking and begin to see ourselves thriving! God wants to bring new inventions and medical breakthroughs.

One thing that sometimes is hard to understand is that when the devil is doing his worst and throwing the worst—that means he knows his days are short, and he is going to try to do as much damage as possible in as little time as possible. Many times when we are in a serious battle, we tend to think that maybe this is it—no need to dream any longer, just survive. Maybe this is when Jesus comes back to get us. However, we need to learn to think "opposites." Understand that the devil is a thermometer to what God is planning to do. God ALWAYS has the final say, so in God's plan, there is always a happy ending to the movie. The bad guy *will be caught* and the good guys will be heroes. Do not think for a moment that when God's people are praying, the devil will be the winner; he is a loser and will always be a loser.

> *He who sits in the heavens shall laugh;*
> *The Lord shall hold them in derision.*
>
> Psalm 2:4

I realize that none of us know exactly the timing of Jesus' return for His Bride; however, knowing the principles of God of divine victory, do you really think we are going to leave this place looking like a pitiful bride? I don't think so. I expect a happy ending to this movie. I expect that God's Church will be amazing before Jesus comes back. We will truly be walking on the high places. We will truly be walking in our spiritual authority. Therefore, just like Jesus declared "it is finished" before he dismissed His spirit on the cross, I believe His Bride will have a "finishing our race" moment, and we will let our Bridegroom know that it is time to come get us! In Revelation 22:17, John records that the Spirit *and* the Bride say "Come." Yes, the Father will make the final decision, but I believe it will be soon afterwards.

> *But none of these things move me; nor do I count my life dear to myself, so that I may **finish my race with joy**, and the ministry which I received from the Lord Jesus, to testify to the gospel of the grace of God.* (emphasis added)
>
> Acts 20:24

As for America, I believe we have an unfinished assignment. We were raised up as the most powerful nation in the world to be an example of a nation with a covenant with God. Israel has a covenant with God and America's forefathers dedicated this nation to God and therefore, we also have a covenant with God. I believe God wants our latter glory to far outshine our former glory. This of course is not to be better than any other nation or people, but Jesus said the greatest among you will serve. I believe God wants us to be a nation that spreads liberty and justice—that we help others be free and that we spread the gospel around the world. If we pray and ask God, He promised to heal our land:

> *...if My people who are called by My name will humble themselves, and pray and seek My face, and turn from their wicked ways, then I will hear from heaven, and will forgive their sin and heal their land.*
>
> 2 Chronicles 7:14

As we continue to pray for our nation, I believe our nation will be healed as well as become a conduit of healing over other nations. The phrase that is printed and engraved on our money, IN GOD WE TRUST, should continue to be our motto!

── When Our Enemies Are No More ──

> *For evildoers shall be cut off;*
> *but those who wait on the Lord,*
> *they shall inherit the earth.*
> *For yet a little while and the wicked*
>   *shall be no more;*
> *indeed, you will look carefully for his place,*
> *but it shall be no more.*
> *But the meek shall inherit the earth,*

> *and shall delight themselves*
> *in the abundance of peace.*
> Psalm 37:9–11

The above verse is what is about to happen in America and around the world. The Lord has been giving me this verse for some time. Think about it for a moment. We already know there will be no enemies in heaven, nor will there be any after Jesus comes back and judges the wicked. So for a promise like that to be given, I believe God is saying that the verse above can be possible on this side of heaven. Think about the story in 2 Chronicles 20 when Jehoshaphat and Israel were surrounded by enemies and God said you will not need to fight in this battle:

> *You will not need to fight in this battle. Position yourselves, stand still and see the salvation of the Lord, who is with you, O Judah and Jerusalem! Do not fear or be dismayed; tomorrow go out against them, for the Lord is with you.*
> 2 Chronicles 20:17

We must position ourselves for victory and know that God is with us! I love how in verse 24 of this chapter, the Bible records that *there were no enemies left!* Like I said earlier, this does not necessarily mean that our enemies are *physically* gone, but I believe God is saying that their positions of control and power over us will be removed!

So therefore, until Jesus comes back, yes, we will still have battles (Ephesians 6), and the devil will still be around. However, we can come to a place of walking in the promises of protection in Psalm 91 where no enemies can touch us! I believe that we can believe that for our personal lives and for our nation. Prayer changes things, and we are in a place where we are going to see God wipe out a whole bunch of spiritual enemies at one time.

This is truly going to be "The Day of the Saints." Prophet Bill Hamon wrote a book with that title in 2012. My husband and I have that book, and it was very encouraging and influential in our lives. In a nutshell, Prophet Hamon was seeing in the future a day where the Church would be outside the four walls of a building, influencing all aspects of society. This is that day! God is about to do a divine flip, so saints, be ready to take your mountain.

The devil has had his final say over America, and we are about to see God's voice and hand move like we have never seen before. We must run with it and not ever again let someone or a group of people take our liberty away. This is a "WE THE PEOPLE" country!

The Role of Reformers

When our rightful President, Donald Trump, is back in office, and the corrupt administration has been put out, we need to be prepared to take ground in every area. Donald Trump, his family, and his administration cannot do that alone. Just like when David took out Goliath (did the hardest part for Israel), we need to take out the rest of the Philistines (again, I'm not talking physical war here but spiritual). We need to work to see unrighteous laws changed. We need to see our school systems reformed. We need to see entertainment reformed. We need to see business laws be reformed. I believe God will bring His people into prosperity by making it easier for us to succeed. I see a day where we will have more rich people than poor because of the goodness of the Lord in this place. This will be our testimony:

> *Then it shall be to Me a name of joy, a praise, and an honor before all nations of the earth, who shall hear all the good that I do to them; they shall fear and tremble for all the goodness and all the prosperity that I provide for it.*
>
> Jeremiah 33:9

What are reformers? Reformers are people who dedicate themselves to bring needed reform (change) in society, the Church, or any other area. Here are a few definitions of reform:[1]

Noun:
— the improvement or amendment of what is wrong, corrupt, unsatisfactory, etc.
— an instance of this

Verb:
— to change to a better state, form, etc.; improve by alteration, substitution, abolition, etc.
— to cause (a person) to abandon wrong or evil ways of life or conduct.
— to put an end to (abuses, disorders, etc.).

We need to ask God what our part in the reformation will be. In what areas do you see injustices and need for reformation that causes a passion in you? We need to get involved at local levels and allow church to be everyday life for us. I believe we will be a nation of reformers!

As I mentioned previously in chapter two, one of my favorite Church reformers is Martin Luther, who was famous for bringing back the truth that salvation is by grace and not by works in the early 1500s. Much of the Church world at that time had gone far out of the range of true biblical teachings and had put the people in much bondage to legalistic traditions set by religious leaders. Luther brought great reform to the Church world and is still celebrated today as a great reformer who set multitudes free from false doctrines to understand the true gospel of grace that Jesus died to give His Church.

I believe Donald Trump is an example of a political reformer and a political prophet. He has been raised up for such a time as this to bring much needed reformation to our government. He and his family have gone through very serious persecution and threats; however, God is protecting Donald Trump along with his family and his team, and they will complete their assignment. There are many of you reading this who will feel called to help in some way in this effort.

Moving from the Old Wineskin to the New

In order to go to the new place, we have to leave the old place. I know—this is deep! When Abraham was told to go to a new land, the Bible records:

> *Now the Lord had said to Abram:*
> *"Get out of your country,*

> *from your family*
> *and from your father's house,*
> *to a land that I will show you.*
> *I will make you a **great nation**;*
> *I will bless you*
> *and make your name great;*
> *and you shall be a blessing."* (emphasis added)
> Genesis 12:1–2

It is a blessing from God to make "a great nation." In Abraham's case he had to physically move to a new location. However, the point I want to make here is that we have to leave old, defeated mindsets and move to one of new dreams of victory. God knew that Abraham couldn't move fully in the new land while he was still living in the old. Jesus told the people they must replace their old wineskins with new:

> *And no one puts new wine into old wineskins; or else the new wine bursts the wineskins, the wine is spilled, and the wineskins are ruined. But new wine must be put into new wineskins.*
> Mark 2:22

Jesus was teaching the Jews that in order to move to the new and better covenant He was bringing them into, they must first leave the old wineskins and replace them with the new. This is true for what God is about to bring about in our nation and world. He is removing old wineskins right now. Politically, that will mean removing old ways of corruption and politics as usual in order for us to have fresh new leadership and ways of running this country that honors God and serves the people. In many cases this will mean the removal of the elite establishment (the Sauls) that are accustomed to having their own set of rules that don't apply to us. God wants to bring in new leaders with a spirit of David, who love our nation and love the people.

For us as individuals, we need to remove the old wineskins of surviving and move to the new wineskin of thriving. Remember, we are the head and not the tail! We are in an Esther moment of favor and great positions of influence. Get rid of the old mindsets of 'it won't get any better than this'! Yes, it will, because God has promised us He is about to do something amazing! We need to renew our mindsets for victory. God's ways are always the best.

——— Dream Big ———————————

I have always loved the song, *"Dream Big,"* released by The Martins in 1998. God will play that song in my mind sometimes when I need to be encouraged and stretched in faith. Here are some of the lyrics of this amazing song:

> *I believe that anything is possible*
> *If we understand who Jesus is*
>
> *I believe there's nothing that can stop us*
> *If we learn to dream like Jesus did*
>
> *So don't limit your ambition*
> *To what's commonly defined*
> *God has a special heart*
> *For those who walk outside the line*
> *Don't be afraid to spread your wings and fly*
> *It doesn't hurt to try*

> *If you're gonna dream…*
>
> *Dream big*
> *It's the Lord's desire for you to*
> *Dream big*
> *In everything you say and do*
> *You'll see your greatest dream come true*
> *'Cause all of Heaven is dreaming big for you*

Remember that all things are possible. Let's believe for witty inventions (Proverbs 8:12 KJV). Let's believe for medical breakthroughs. Let's believe for even better energy resources. I love the following verse:

> *Call to Me, and I will answer you, and show you great and mighty things, which you do not know.*
>
> Jeremiah 33:3

There is no problem that God cannot give us a solution for. Don't believe that all the cool inventions have been created already. God always saves the best for last! A biblical example of this is when Jesus turned the water into wine at the wedding in Cana of Galilee (John 2:1–12):

> *When the master of the feast had tasted the water that was made wine, and did not know where it came from (but the servants who had drawn the water knew), the master of the feast called the bridegroom. And he said to him, "Every man at the beginning sets out the good wine, and when the guests have well*

> *drunk, then the inferior. You have kept the good wine until now!"*
>
> John 2:9–10

In the story above when Jesus turned the water into wine, He created wine that was better than any of the wine they had previously at the wedding. I believe this is an example of what God wants to do in our nation and many other nations. No matter how good things have been in past times, God wants us to believe for *better*—better government, better schools, better economy, better inventions, better quality of life and so forth.

Also, this story of the wedding started out with some important prophetic significance: *"On the third day…"* (John 2:1). There are no insignificant details in God's Word! The third day, as I pointed out in chapter five, is significant since we are in the third millennium since Jesus was resurrected. Also, America is in her third century since our birth in 1776! This third century will be America's best century so far!

We are about to enter the promised land on earth and see the warfare be quieted for a season, so let's take advantage of the victories we are about to get and make great strides to glorify God in every area of society.

The Glory of God over This Nation and the Earth

Many ministers have declared that God is about to bring "His glory" over the earth. I totally believe this. We are about to enter into an Isaiah 60 moment:

> *Arise, shine;*
> *For your light has come!*
> *And the glory of the Lord is risen upon you.*
> *For behold, the darkness shall cover the earth,*
> *And deep darkness the people;*
> *But the Lord will arise over you,*
> *And His glory will be seen upon you.*
> *The Gentiles shall come to your light,*
> *And kings to the brightness of your rising.*
> Isaiah 60:1–3

Revival will sweep across our nation and this earth. Look up, for we are entering a new day. Glory will come and God's presence will be poured out on the earth. Prepare yourself and dream again, for the best is yet to come!

> *When the Lord brought back the captivity of Zion,*
> *we were like those who dream.*
> *Then our mouth was filled with laughter,*
> *and our tongue with singing.*
> *Then they said among the nations,*
> *"The Lord has done great things for them."*
> *The Lord has done great things for us,*
> *And we are glad.*
> Psalm 126:1–3

This will be the testimony of the United States of America after God does a complete restoration in our government and all society. This will be the testimony of God's people around the world. This will be the testimony of many nations. May God richly bless the United States of America, and may you believe this for your country also!

I will end with these words that powerfully rose up within me recently. I believe God is saying this to our nation:

It's time to arise,
   my beloved America!

Receive the favor God has for you,
      O United States of America.

This is a new day for you.

So I say to you,

ARISE!

Bibliography

Chapter 1: My Beloved America

1. Kunneman, Hank. "Prophecy: Pay Attention To The First Six Months Of 2022." *Hank + Brenda,* December 31, 2021, https://hankandbrenda.org/prophecy-pay-attention-to-the-first-six-months-of-2022/
2. Kunneman, Hank. "Prophecy - Plagues, 2020 Decade, Harsh Start, Then Rest." *Hank + Brenda,* September 5, 2019, https://hankandbrenda.org/prophecy-plagues-2020-decade-harsh-start-then-rest/

⸺Chapter 2: The Arising of the Army of God!

1. *Collins English Dictionary*, 13th edition, s.v. "arise"
2. Rick Joyner, *The Second American Revolution/Civil War* (Fort Mill: MorningStar, 2021).
3. *Hitchcock's Bible Names Dictionary,* s.v. "Gideon."
4. *Hitchcock's Bible Names Dictionary,* s.v. "Midian."
5. Merrill Chapin Tenney, *Zondervan Pictorial Encyclopedia of the Bible,* vol. 1, *A – C,* (Grand Rapids: Zondervan Publishing House, 1975).
6. Joyce Meyer, *Do It Afraid: Embracing Courage in the Face of Fear* (New York: FaithWords, 2020).
7. *Hitchcock's Bible Names Dictionary,* s.v. "Amalek."

⸺Chapter 4: Restoring Our Voices⸺

1. Joyce Meyer, *Do It Afraid: Embracing Courage in the Face of Fear* (New York: FaithWords, 2020).
2. Katie Reilly, "Read Hillary Clinton's 'Basket of Deplorables' Remarks About Donald Trump Supporters," *Times,* September 10, 2016, https://time.com/4486502/hillary-clinton-basket-of-deplorables-transcript/.
3. Alliance Defending Freedom, "Jack is Back in Court, Again. Enough is Enough," *Alliance Defending Freedom,* https://adflegal.org/enough-is-enough.
4. *The New Strong's Exhaustive Concordance of the Bible,* 3954.
5. Thomas Nelson, *The Holy Bible, New King James Version* (Nashville: Thomas Nelson, 1982).

6. Dutch Sheets, *Authority in Prayer: Praying with Power and Purpose* (Minneapolis: Bethany House, 2006).

CHAPTER 5: THE THIRD DAY ERA

1. James M. Freeman, *Manners and Customs of the Bible: A Complete Guide to the Origin and Significance of Our Time-Honored Biblical Tradition* (Plainfield: Logos International, 1972), 532.
2. *Hitchcock's Bible Names Dictionary*, s.v. "Vashti."
3. *The New Strong's Exhaustive Concordance of the Bible*, 3341.
4. *Hitchcock's Bible Names Dictionary*, s.v. "Esther."
5. *Hitchcock's Bible Names Dictionary*, s.v. "Mordecai."
6. *School of Revival*, Jen Miskov, School of Revival, 2020, https://www.schoolofrevivalfire.com/.
7. Gary M. Galles, "17 Benjamin Franklin Quotes on Tyranny, Liberty, and Human Rights," *FEE: Foundation for Economic Education*, January 27, 2020, https://fee.org/articles/17-benjamin-franklin-quotes-on-tyranny-liberty-and-rights/.
8. Kash Patel, interview by Steve Shultz, *Prophets and Patriots*, The Elijah List, June 14, 2022, https://rumble.com/v18f95h-prophets-and-5-with-kash-patel-and-steve-shultz.html.
9. *Hitchcock's Bible Names Dictionary*, s.v. "Haman."
10. *Hitchcock's Bible Names Dictionary*, s.v. "Hammedatha."
11. *Hitchcock's Bible Names Dictionary*, s.v. "Agag."
12. "Woman screams as Donald Trump is sworn in as President," YouTube video, 1:08, posted by "On Demand

News," January 21, 2017, https://www.youtube.com/watch?v=wDYNVH0U3cs.
13. Bernard Kirk, "Democrats desperately push the 'peaceful protestors' delusion," *The Hill*, August 21, 2020, https://thehill.com/opinion/criminal-justice/513063-democrats-desperately-push-the-peaceful-protesters-delusion/.
14. Tommy Tenney, *Finding Favor with the King: Preparing for Your Moment in His Presence* (Bloomington: Bethany House Publishers, 2003), 127.
15. 2000 Mules, directed by Dinesh D'Souza (Salem Media Group, 2022), DVD.
16. *Hitchcock's Bible Names Dictionary*, s.v. "Adar."
17. *The New Strong's Exhaustive Concordance of the Bible*, 5437.

Chapter 6: Choosing Greatness

1. Charlene Aaron, "Lance Wallnau: Witches Trying to Bind Trump for Fear That God Will Work Through Him," *CBN News*, April 9, 2017, https://www1.cbn.com/cbnnews/us/2017/april/lance-wallnau-witches-want-to-bind-trump-for-fear-that-god-will-work-through-him.
2. Lance Wallnau, *God's Chaos Candidate: Donald J. Trump and the American Unraveling* (Keller: Killer Sheep Media, 2016).
3. "Half Shekel Cyrus Trump Temple Coin," Temple Coins, last modified 2022, https://www.temple-coins.com/products/half-shekel-cyrus-trump-temple-coin.
4. "Donald," *Behind the Name*, Mike Campbell, last modified January 21, 2022, https://www.behindthename.com/name/donald.

— Bibliography —

5. *Hitchcock's Bible Names Dictionary*, s.v. "John."
6. "Trump," babynames.com, last modified 2022, https://babynames.com/name/trump.
7. Johnny Enlow, interview by Steve Shultz, *Elijah Streams*, The Elijah List, 2020, https://fb.watch/hwCt4vpzdi/.
8. "Trump mercilessly mocks Biden's 'Great MAGA King' slam," YouTube video, 4:18, posted by "Sky News Australia," May 13, 2022, https://www.youtube.com/watch?v=S9W9hDYB9gA.
9. "Joseph Prince - God's Blueprint For Leadership - 18 Jul 18," YouTube video, 5:56, posted by "Joseph Prince," September 6, 2018, https://www.youtube.com/watch?v=yD5uj66eKXk.
10. Katie Reilly, "Read Hillary Clinton's 'Basket of Deplorables' Remarks About Donald Trump Supporters," *Times*, September 10, 2016, https://time.com/4486502/hillary-clinton-basket-of-deplorables-transcript/.
11. *Collins English Dictionary*, 13th edition, s.v. "deplorable."
12. NBC News, "Full text: President Trump's 2020 RNC acceptance speech," *NBC News*, August 28, 2020, https://www.nbcnews.com/politics/2020-election/read-full-text-president-donald-trump-s-acceptance-speech-rnc-n1238636.
13. Tara Law, "Read the Full Transcript of President Trump's State of the Union Address," *Time*, February 5, 2019, https://time.com/5521860/2019-state-of-the-union-trump-transcript/.

Chapter 7: Gathering Together on the Wall

1. *Hitchcock's Bible Names Dictionary*, s.v. "Hanani."
2. *Hitchcock's Bible Names Dictionary*, s.v. "Sanballat."
3. *Smith's Bible Dictionary*, s.v. "Tobiah."

Chapter 8: The Tale of Two Towers

1. Post Editorial Board, "The Steele dossier's tawdry, absurd and fake 'sources'," *New York Post*, May 11, 2022, https://nypost.com/2022/05/11/the-steele-dossiers-tawdry-absurd-and-fake-sources/.
2. *Hitchcock's Bible Names Dictionary*, s.v. "Babel."
3. *Collins English Dictionary*, 13th edition, s.v. "carnal."

Chapter 9: The Day of the Prophets

1. *The Elijah List*, Elijah List Ministries, accessed 2022, https://www.elijahlist.com/index.php.
2. Charlene Aaron, "Lance Wallnau: Witches Trying to Bind Trump for Fear That God Will Work Through Him," *CBN News*, April 9, 2017, https://www1.cbn.com/cbnnews/us/2017/april/lance-wallnau-witches-want-to-bind-trump-for-fear-that-god-will-work-through-him.

— Bibliography —

——Chapter 10: Riding on the Mountaintops with Jesus——

1. Donna Rigney, interview by Steve Shultz, *Elijah Streams*, The Elijah List, October 25, 2022, https://rumble.com/v1ps5yh-donna-rigney-watch-and-see-my-arm-of-justice-fall.html.
2. Douglas Harper, "Dis-," *Online Etymology Dictionary*, 2022, https://www.etymonline.com/word/dis-

——Chapter 11: True Liberty——

1. *The New Strong's Exhaustive Concordance of the Bible*, 4739.
2. *Random House Unabridged Dictionary*, 2nd edition, s.v. "standfast."
3. Jennifer Wishon, "'We the People' Are All Criminals: If You Live in the US and Are Over 18, You're Guilty," *CBN News*, September 9, 2018, https://www1.cbn.com/cbnnews/us/2018/september/if-you-live-in-the-us-and-are-over-age-18-youre-probably-a-criminal.

——Chapter 12: The Rebirth of America——

1. *Collins English Dictionary*, 13th edition, s.v. "reform."

Acknowledgements

First, I want to thank my Lord and Savior, Jesus Christ, who changed my life radically at the age of eighteen. He is truly the one that *"I live and move and have my being"* and wouldn't want to live for one second without Him.

Second, I want to thank my husband, Jim, who has been a champion and encourager for me along with our three children: Ashley, Rebecca, and Kaleb. Jim has helped with a bit of everything from artistic inspiration, editing, prayer, to being a shoulder to cry on when I felt overwhelmed! I couldn't have done this without the amazing support I have at home. I am so thankful to have a family as wonderful, loving, and talented as you!

Next, I want to thank my two closest friends and prayer partners of many years, Judy Taylor and Evelyn Cutler. We have journeyed through life together, and I'm so grateful God placed you both in my life! I would not be who I am today without the love, input, support, and prayers that we have had together.

Also, I want to thank my dear friend, Christy Kendrick, who I have known since I was in my 20's. She is an author herself and has encouraged and prayed for me and this book project for several years, for which I am so grateful!

In 2020, God opened some amazing doors that connected me with many Christian friends and leaders around the world (which I told the story of in chapter five of this book) that have been a spiritual support and family to me. Many of these friends have prayed and prophesied over me and this book; their love and support has carried me through to the finishing line, and for that, I'm forever grateful! Special thanks to:

—*The School of Revival Family* and *The Writing in the Glory Family,* both founded by Jennifer Miskov, Ph.D., who is a revival historian, author, and writing coach. Her *Writing in the Glory* classes gave me many of the tools I needed in finishing this project. I have made many dear friends in these groups who have prayed for me and this project!

—*Kingdom Clarity Family,* founded by Ruth Saw, who is an author, mentor, and writing coach. Ruth Saw is anointed to encourage and pray people into their destinies. Aja McCombs, who helps lead this group, is a very anointed intercessor and prophet whose words and prayers have been life changing to me. This family has been a very key part of delivering this baby, and I love and appreciate you guys so much!

—*Sisterhood of Grace,* founded by Ruthann Miller, an author and leader who has helped countless women find their identity and healing in Jesus. This group lives up to their name: their love, prayers, and support have made a great difference in my life!

Also, I want to give thanks to some special people that I met in the above groups who have been such a blessing in my life and in this writing process:

—Gabby Heusser, *Author, Evangelist, and President of "Gabby Heusser Ministries."* Gabby's passion for the Lord spreads joy and love to all around her. Gabby has been such a special friend who has mentored and walked closely with me through the finishing process of this book.

—Hacksun and Seya Cha, *Traveling Missionaries.* I bonded with Hacksun and Seya pretty much immediately after I first met them. They have been so supportive and encouraging to me through this process and are like family to me. So proud of the wonderful work they are doing as evangelists, winning countless souls to the Lord!

—Tremonisha Putros, *Author, Teacher.* I met Tremonisha in our writing group. Her encouraging words, prayers, and prophetic words over me brought so much comfort and blessing. Her joy and laughter bring love and peace wherever she goes.

- —Tina Webb, *Author, Podcaster, Minister.* Tina Webb gave me my first ever interview regarding this book before it was even close to being finished! Her belief in me along with her mentorship was such a blessing to me!
- —Kisha Toussaint, *Intercessor, Minister.* Kisha's deep joy and love is contagious to all who meet her. Her unconditional love and friendship in my life is such a treasure and gift from heaven!
- —Luke Whitfield, *Missionary, Minister.* Not long after I met Luke in the *School of Revival*, he had a prophetic word for me that I would have a "global voice." That has been a word that has meant so much to me and has given me so much hope—especially since I've lived in the same state (Georgia) all my life and have done very little traveling!
- —Reina Laaman, *Author, Actress.* I met Reina in a writing group, and she instantly became such a dear friend. Her prophetic words and prayers have meant so much to me!

There is an old saying, "it takes a village," concerning the fact that many times it takes many people coming together to get something done. This has certainly been true for the writing of this book. This vision came to me in a time of prayer about a decade ago, and I'm so grateful that God gave me so many amazing people to pray and prophesy me through this process. There are many other dear friends that have blessed me with prayers and encouragement who are not specifically mentioned here, but know that I am so thankful for you all!